CHILD PSYC

About the Authors

Albert Angrilli received the degree of Doctor of Philosophy from New York University. He also holds degrees in school psychology and guidance, and is a diplomate in school psychology. Dr. Angrilli was a clinical psychologist with child guidance teams of the New York State Department of Mental Hygiene and a consultant school psychologist in a number of schools in upper New York State. He joined the faculty of Queens College of the City University of New York in 1953 and is now a professor in the Department of Graduate Programs in Educational Services. He served as director of the Educational Clinic from 1966 until it closed in 1976. He has been active in presentations to professional and parent groups and is the author of many articles in professional journals. Dr. Angrilli has served on college faculties in Puerto Rico, Israel, and Switzerland. He is also an adjunct professor of psychology in the School of Professional Psychology at the Florida Institute of Technology.

Lucile Helfat received the degree of Master of Social Work from Columbia University and is a member of the Academy of Certified Social Workers. In 1966 she joined the faculty of Queens College of the City University of New York, where she worked in the Educational Clinic and taught graduate and undergraduate courses in child development and educational psychology. Mrs. Helfat has served as consultant to teachers and guidance personnel and has conducted institutes, seminars, and training programs in the field of affective education and preventative mental health. Prior to 1966 she was social work coordinator of Developmental Evaluation Services at Long Island Jewish Medical Center, and she helped organize and run one of the country's first programs in adolescent medicine under sponsorship of the U.S. Department of Health, Education, and Welfare. Mrs. Helfat has contributed to leading professional publications including the *Journal of Clinical Child Psychology,* the *New York State Journal of Medicine,* and *Learning Magazine.*

CHILD PSYCHOLOGY

Albert Angrilli
and
Lucile Helfat

BARNES & NOBLE BOOKS
A DIVISION OF HARPER & ROW, PUBLISHERS
New York, Cambridge, Hagerstown, Philadelphia,
San Francisco, London, Mexico City, São Paulo, Sydney

CHILD PSYCHOLOGY. Copyright © 1981 by Albert Angrilli and Lucile Helfat. All rights reserved. Printed in the United States of America. No part of this book may be used or reproduced in any manner whatsoever without written permission except in the case of brief quotations embodied in critical articles and reviews. For information address Harper & Row, Publishers, Inc., 10 East 53rd Street, New York, N.Y. 10022. Published simultaneously in Canada by Fitzhenry & Whiteside Limited, Toronto.

FIRST EDITION

Designer: Sidney Feinberg

Library of Congress Cataloging in Publication Data

Angrilli, Albert.
  Child psychology.
  Includes bibliographical references and index.
  1. Child psychology.   I. Helfat, Lucile, joint author.   II. Title.
BF721.A676   1981   155.4   80–7764
ISBN 0-06-460189-7

81 82 83 84 85 10 9 8 7 6 5 4 3 2 1

Contents

Preface *vii*

1. The Study of Child Psychology   1

   The Importance of Child Psychology 1
   Historical Review 2
   Methods of Study in Child Psychology 6

2. Principles and Theories of Development   13

   Principles of Development 13
   The Role of Theory in Child Psychology 18
   Theories of Development 19

3. Life Begins: Prenatal and Neonatal Development   30

   Prenatal Development 30
   Birth 41
   Neonatal Development 43

4. Infancy: The First Eighteen Months   49

   Physical Development 50
   Mental Development 53
   Personality Development 61
   Social Development 69

5. Toddlerhood Through the Preschool Years   73

   Physical Development 74
   Mental Development 77

Personality Development 90
Social Development 101

6. The Middle Years   106

   Physical Development 106
   Mental Development 109
   Personality Development 124
   Social Development 128
   Adjustment Problems of Childhood 138

7. Adolescence   143

   Physical Development 144
   Mental Development 146
   Personality Development 148
   Social Development 152
   Adjustment Problems of Adolescence 156
   Growing into Maturity 160

References 163
Index 171

Preface

Child Psychology traces the growth and development of the child from conception through adolescence, presenting in condensed form the standard subject material of courses in child and adolescent psychology. It also reviews the major principles and theories currently being applied to the study of child psychology. This book will be helpful not only to students in psychology courses but also to parents, teachers, and others concerned with child rearing and education.

The subject has been approached chronologically, and the material dealing with each age group summarizes the most widely used textbooks in the field as well as pertinent material from periodicals and research journals. This approach provides students with a framework for study and discussion that will be particularly helpful to those taking a course or using a textbook with a topics approach.

The first two chapters in *Child Psychology* deal with the various theories and principles of child development. Chapter 3 concentrates on the early stages of the life cycle. The following four chapters—Infancy, Toddlerhood Through the Preschool Years, The Middle Years, and Adolescence—are each subdivided into four main topics: physical development, mental development, personality development, and social development. This organization simplifies review of the developmental aspects of each stage and helps the reader recall and supplement other readings on the subject. Bibliographical references provide sources for further study.

In any book on child development the problem of pronouns arises. To avoid the tiresome *he or she*, we have used plural forms where they are appropriate. In more cases than we would like, we have resorted to the generic *he*.

We wish to express our deepest gratitude to our spouses, Alma and Bernard, who helped bring this book to fruition. Minnie Graff of Queens College was helpful to us in so many tangible and intangible ways. We would also like to thank our editor Jeanne Flagg, whose knowledge and skill have given clarity and focus to the book.

ALBERT ANGRILLI
LUCILE HELFAT

CHILD PSYCHOLOGY

1
The Study of Child Psychology

Child psychology, or child development, as it has been called in recent years, is concerned with the changes in human behavior that take place with growth, maturation, and experience. Its goals are the observation, measurement, description, and explanation of behavior at various stages of life, from conception into adulthood.

THE IMPORTANCE OF CHILD PSYCHOLOGY

The unfolding of behavior as various forces act upon the growing child, a fascinating study in itself, draws on and in turn illuminates many areas in the biological and social sciences. On the practical side, child psychology has substantial value for parents and professionals in child rearing and education, and it yields satisfying rewards to society in general and to children in particular.

Help to Parents. Child psychology explores the many facets of the developing child and the effect of early experiences on behavior. Thus it has much to offer parents that will guide them in rearing their children and put them in a better position to avoid or minimize the pitfalls leading to psychological and behavioral problems.

Help to Professionals. The study of child psychology has played an active and significant role in the development of educational practices. The question of how, and even why, children learn has led to specific teaching techniques, learning environments, and approaches to classroom management. Child psychology has also contributed to important changes in pediatric medicine, psychiatry, social work, and other child-related fields. For example, adolescent medicine has emerged as a medical specialty in recognition of the specific psychological needs of children who are in the transitional period between childhood and adulthood. Similarly, the specialty of child psychiatry developed to understand and work with the psychological problems of children.

Benefits to Society. A great many social problems have their roots in, or are intertwined with, the psychology of children. Youthful violence, drug abuse, and juvenile delinquency are a few of the problems that may be better understood through psychological study. Appropriate and effective measures may then be taken to lessen or alleviate the damage to society.

Benefits to Children. While it is almost too obvious to mention, the principal beneficiary of the study of psychology is the child. Improved understanding of children leads to a better growing and learning environment and, as a result, a better chance at a happy and productive life.

HISTORICAL REVIEW

The systematic study of children is a relative newcomer to the roster of sciences in the Western world. Only in recent times has childhood been considered to be a distinct stage of life.

The Child in Ancient Times. The ancients had little interest in children as children; they thought of them primarily in terms of their economic value (5). Although the ancient philosophers did not concern themselves with child development, Plato, in *The Republic*, proposed state-controlled communes to train children in the direction of their aptitudes. Aristotle also recognized that children have different potentialities; his suggestion was to strengthen the family unit.

The Child in Medieval Times. In the Middle Ages, children were dressed and treated as miniature adults. They worked in the fields and in the home, and were apprenticed. Those who attended school did so along with adults. After babyhood, children were not given special care or protection. They joined adults in gambling and drinking, and, given the crowded sleeping conditions, they were free to observe sexual activities (2).

The Changing View of the Child: Seventeenth to Eighteenth Centuries. It was not until the seventeenth century that childhood was considered to be a separate stage and children were thought to need special treatment (12). By 1600, children wore clothing distinct from that of adults. No longer did they participate in adult activities such as betting, or study in classes along with adults. The Reformation and Counter Reformation had their impact on the moral and ethical training of children. These movements gave increasing importance to schools as institutions for instilling in children the currently accepted moral values. Such philosophers and educational thinkers as John Amos Comenius, John Locke, and Jean Jacques Rousseau directed attention to various aspects of childhood.

COMENIUS. In his publications *School of Infancy* (1628) and *The World in Pictures* (1654), John Amos Comenius presented children as individuals with special interests and abilities, rather than as immature adults.

LOCKE. In the late seventeenth century, the English philosopher John Locke wrote that the child is born with a mind like a blank slate, a tabula rasa, upon which all subsequent learning and experience become imprinted (8). He believed in individualized instruction and in the concept of reward and punishment to teach self-control and self-denial.

ROUSSEAU. In the book *Emile,* published in 1762, Jean Jacques Rousseau analyzed the educational needs of children from a completely different point of view (10). Rousseau theorized that children had an innate sense of right and wrong and therefore should be permitted to learn at their own pace and through their own experience. Many of his ideas were later incorporated into the progressive education movement.

The Emergence of Child Psychology. Child psychology as a separate discipline had its roots in the informal biographies of children. More systematic studies followed. Most of the early studies were based on observations of individual children.

BABY BIOGRAPHERS. Biographical observations and studies of their own children were published in the eighteenth century by Johann Heinrich Pestalozzi and Dieterich Tiedemann, and in the nineteenth century by Wilhelm Preyer and Charles Darwin. Darwin's publication of *On the Origin of Species* in 1859 has been described as "probably the single most vital force in the establishment of child psychology as a scientific discipline" (9, p. 13) because it focused attention on the study of man's origins, including his childhood. Darwin published his *Biographical Sketch of an Infant* later in his career, in 1877 (3).

G. STANLEY HALL. The understanding of children and the problems of childhood were advanced by pioneering studies undertaken by G. Stanley Hall. Hall, in order to determine "the contents of children's minds," sent questionnaires to teachers and parents that were designed to elicit recollections of childhood memories (6, pp. 139–173). This technique helped the study of child psychology develop in a more objective and scientific manner. Building upon his analysis of parents' observations of their growing children, Hall, working at Clark University, laid down many of the basic principles of child psychology. From the *Boston Kindergarten Studies* of 1880 until his death in 1924, Hall devoted himself to proving that the study of development was central to the problem of understanding human beings.

FRANCIS GALTON. Galton began his studies of human intelligence in the mid-1800s. Throughout his work he emphasized the recognition of individual differences and the need to measure them. Galton's introduction of statistical tools for mental measurement lay the groundwork for the mental measurement and intelligence testing movement of the early twentieth century.

ALFRED BINET AND THEOPHILE SIMON. In 1905 Alfred Binet and Theophile Simon, working with French children, developed what was to become the classic intelligence test. Lewis Terman, at Stanford University, later produced the Stanford version of the Binet-Simon test, the Stanford-Binet Intelligence Test (13). This instrument has become one of the standard tests used in assessing the intelligence of children in schools throughout the United States. Thus, the study of child psychology became intertwined with the mental measurements movement and the evolving discipline of educational psychology.

ARNOLD GESELL. The study and scientific observation of the child as a developing, growing, and behaving being became a central factor in the evolution of child psychology. Arnold Gesell, a student of G. Stanley Hall at Clark University and, later, a graduate of Yale University School of Medicine, studied child development and concluded that the behavioral patterns of children paralleled their physical growth and unfolded in an orderly way. His stages of development have served as gospel for generations of parents and contributed greatly to the recognition of child psychology (4).

JOHN B. WATSON. The 1920s saw the emergence of John B. Watson's "behaviorism" as a dominant psychological force in child rearing (14). Borrowing from the work of Pavlov, who had demonstrated that a dog could be taught to respond to a stimulus by creating an association between it and another stimulus, Watson developed the theory that children could be similarly controlled. Watson's ideas were incorporated into early child-rearing manuals published by the United States government and have led to such current thinking in psychology as B. F. Skinner's concept of operant conditioning and the Behavior Modification approach to learning.

Such educators as John Dewey and Maria Montessori became interested in the learning processes of children. "How do they learn, and how do we teach them?" were the basic questions to be answered.

JOHN DEWEY. Dewey, a philosopher whose ideas on education led to the progressive education movement, stressed the value of personal experience in learning. Reacting to the rigid teaching methods of the day, he urged educators to encourage children to be curious and "learn by doing."

MARIA MONTESSORI. In the early 1900s, in Rome, Maria Montessori established nursery schools for disadvantaged children that were based on individual discovery through the use of special learning materials. The Montessori method anticipated many of the programmed learning techniques in use in the United States today.

Improvement in the Status of Children. The changing nature of society in the late nineteenth and early twentieth centuries led to the improved status of children and gave further impetus to the establishment of the study of child psychology. As machines began to replace hand labor, children became less valuable as wage earners. It became increasingly evident that upward mobility was in part related to literacy and formal education. This recognition put a premium upon extending to all children the types and scope of schooling that heretofore had been reserved for the children of the more affluent classes. With the emergence of the economic middle class, and with the increase in public education, the period of child dependency and protection was extended far beyond the tender age of six or seven years which for so long had been the limit among the poorer classes. This change, in turn, resulted in greater family cohesion and parental concern for children. As parents became more deeply involved in the health and welfare of their children they turned for guidance to experts such as Watson and Gesell. This interest in what was coming to be known by the public as child psychology became a substantial factor in the popularization of the work of Sigmund Freud and other psychoanalytic clinicians such as Alfred Adler and Carl Jung. On the other hand, the changing status of children within the family was in part responsible for drawing the attention of Freud and his followers to the study of the personality, with all its implications for child rearing.

At present, child psychologists are undertaking many studies in such varied areas as drug addiction, intellectual ability, academic achievement, the development of cognition, and psychosexual identification. Such scientists and scholars as Lawrence Kohlberg, Harry Harlow, Erik Erikson, and Jean Piaget have contributed significantly to the current literature in the field. Their work along with that of others mentioned in this chapter will be discussed more fully in later chapters of this book.

METHODS OF STUDY IN CHILD PSYCHOLOGY

The study of children as a scientific discipline emerged in the early twentieth century as a number of forces converged: changing social conditions, the success of the scientific method, and the recognition of childhood as a distinct stage of life. Intuitive and subjective speculations, based on personal experiences and reflections, gave way to a systematic study of more objective facts and observations from many sources. Child psychologists around the turn of the century began to adapt to their own purposes many of the methods used in the study of the physical sciences. Consequently, at the present time, investigators in child psychology utilize a great many different methods and techniques. These range from the old informal, subjective techniques, which are still useful in certain studies, to approaches characterized by careful experimentation and statistical analysis.

Introspective Reportage. This technique relies on memories, sensations, and experiences, past and present, reported by the subjects. Psychoanalysis leans heavily on this method.

Observations and Biographies. These sources of information are the reports of persons other than the individuals who are the subjects of the study. They may include informal and unsystematic anecdotal observations or careful longitudinal studies which note behavior over a lengthy period of time. Observations are, of course, part of clinical and experimental studies.

Clinical Methods. This approach includes many different procedures, including interviews, case studies, and psychometric techniques, and can be applied in a standardized or nonstandardized way.

INTERVIEWS. These may be formal and informal.

CASE STUDIES. All available personal and social data relating to an individual child, including observations and biographies, are brought together in order to understand the child and his problems.

PSYCHOMETRIC TECHNIQUES. These techniques include questionnaires, rating scales, intelligence tests, achievement tests, aptitude and interest surveys, and tests to evaluate personality characteristics. Among the latter are such projective tests as the Rorschach inkblots, the Thematic Apperception Test, and Figure Drawing tests.

Experimental Methods. Experimental procedures are the essence of scientific methodology. In its pure form, the experimental method sets up controlled conditions and defines specific variables for study. Hypotheses are formulated and tested, and the findings are subjected to statistical analysis. By these means the investigator attempts to exclude conscious or unconscious bias from affecting the outcome of the research. Psychological theories examined and developed by experimental methods may in turn lead to prediction and change.

INDEPENDENT AND DEPENDENT VARIABLES. In designing an experiment, the investigator designates one characteristic, condition, or quality in the study as the *independent variable*. This is the aspect of the study which will be systematically manipulated to test a particular hypothesis. Other variables in the experiment remain constant. For example, an investigator wishing to study the effect of background music on examination-taking by fourth graders will construct a situation in which music will be played during some examinations, but not during others. The same class will be used during the course of the experiment. The subject matter of the test and the time of day will be controlled so that over a period of a term the children will take the same number of tests on the same topics, with or without background music. The differences in achievement under these varying conditions will then be noted. In this oversimplified illustration, the background music, the variable chosen for manipulation, is the independent variable. The average increase or decrease in test scores is the *dependent variable,* because any changes would be assumed to be dependent on the presence or absence of background music.

EXPERIMENTAL AND CONTROL GROUPS. In the above illustration one fourth-grade class was studied over a period of one term to investigate the effect of music on test scores. At times, however, it may be necessary or more desirable to study two different groups, using the same independent variable. In such designs, one group is exposed to the experimental condition, while another matched group is simply identified, but not subjected to any manipulation. At the end of the experiment the two groups are examined to determine the extent of statistically significant differences that occurred as a result of the study. Such differences are then assumed to have been caused by the manipulation of the independent variable. The group exposed to the experimental condition is called the *experimental group* and the matched group is called the *control group.* In the example cited, the investigator could have selected one fourth-grade class as the experimental group (music with examinations) and another fourth-grade class in the same school, matched for ability, achievement level, age, sex, etc., as a control group (no music with examinations). Teacher characteristics and curriculum would be similar for both groups. Any difference in test scores between the groups at the end of the study would be attributed to the effect of the independent variable, background music.

Settings for Child Studies. Investigations in child psychology are carried out in natural or laboratory settings.

NATURAL SETTING. Investigation takes place in the child's normal environment—in the home, the neighborhood, or the school. The study may involve investigation of play, family interaction, or classroom performance, but only a limited degree of controlled manipulation of the child's surroundings is feasible. For example, books or blocks may be introduced into a child's home in order to study the effects of environmental enrichment on intellectual development.

NATURAL EXPERIMENT. Another type of study which also does not attempt to manipulate the child's environment is called the natural experiment. Situations for study are sought out wherein the independent variable occurs naturally. Evaluation of the effect of maternal deprivation on the development of certain children known to have suffered neglect in their early lives would be an example of such a study. The dependent variables may be intellectual, emotional, physical, or social changes due to maternal deprivation.

LABORATORY SETTING. The laboratory setting is so designated because the experiment takes place in an environment specifically designed for research. Equipment might include one-way vision mirrors, control panels, scales, and other monitoring devices. Independent variables can be selected and manipulated systematically under controlled circumstances in a laboratory, and changes can be fully monitored and measured with precision.

Approaches to Child Study. There are two principal approaches to the study of child development: longitudinal studies and cross-sectional studies.

LONGITUDINAL APPROACH. In this method, the subjects under investigation are studied and observed for an extended period of time. For example, a selected group of premature infants may be examined, observed, or tested periodically so that the variables under examination (e.g., height, weight, general health, intelligence) can be noted as the children reach progressively advancing months and years of age. The findings of such investigations may then be generalized to the larger group from which the subjects were drawn and of which they are assumed to be a representative sample. The results of a longitudinal study of a relatively small group of middle-class premature infants may then be said to apply, with caution, to middle-class premature infants in general.

Advantages

1. Reflects developmental changes with greater accuracy because the same child is examined at each time period.
2. Reveals the impact of early events on behavior at later stages.
3. Shows the stability of a given behavior in a particular child.
4. Permits the investigator to readily isolate characteristics under study and control or eliminate contaminating factors.

Disadvantages

1. Such studies are time-consuming, expensive, and unable to provide data on demand. Financial support for remedial programs often requires immediate corroborative evidence; authorities cannot wait for long-term findings.
2. Unforeseen events may invalidate the study. During the course of even a five-year study, some of the children are likely to move away beyond the purview of the investigation. Illness and death may further diminish the number of children in the original sample. To-

ward the end of a long-term study, the key researchers may no longer be involved.

3. The child's life may be affected by the study, which in turn may influence and distort the results. Parents who know that their children will be reexamined in six months or a year may treat them differently than they otherwise would.

4. Cultural changes may limit or invalidate the conclusions. Behavioral patterns for a given age group often differ significantly from one generation to another.

5. New understanding of child behavior and recently devised testing instruments may diminish the value of the early years of study.

CROSS-SECTIONAL APPROACH. In contradistinction to the longitudinal approach, cross-sectional studies compare representative samples of age groups "in the present," not over an extended period. The effect of prematurity on height and weight, for example, might be studied by examining seven groups of premature babies of specified ages, each group consisting of five boys and five girls born of middle-class parents. Group I would consist of ten infants between five and six months of age; Group II, between eleven and thirteen months of age; Group III, seventeen to nineteen months; and so forth. The height and weight of each child would be compared to those in growth tables of children of middle-class parentage in comparable age groups who were not born prematurely. The results would then be generalized, again with caution, to all prematurely born infants of middle-class parentage.

Advantages

1. The results are immediately available. In a relatively short time, behavior differences can be studied for a wide range of ages.

Disadvantages

1. Does not reveal the impact of early events on subsequent behavior.

2. Does not show the stability of a given behavior of a particular child.

3. The sample, or cross-section chosen for study, may not be representative of the larger population.

4. When age-related variables are studied, one age group may

differ subtly but markedly from the others. As a result, the growth transition of the variables under study from age to age may not be accurately reflected. Investigators often have difficulty in matching groups in every characteristic that can influence the variables in a study. Whitehurst and Vasta, to illustrate this, cite a study of the effect of increasing age on intellectual skills (15). A cross-sectional study of fifty-year-olds and seventy-year-olds revealed a lower level of intellectual functioning in the older group, leading to the conclusion that intellectual ability deteriorates with advancing age. When, however, the fifty-year-old group was retested later in life, no significant loss of intellect was noted. The discrepancy may be accounted for by the different composition of the two groups, the different period in which each lived at a particular age, and the differences in their educational backgrounds.

CROSS-SECTIONAL/LONGITUDINAL APPROACH. The study cited immediately above as an illustration of one of the defects in the cross-sectional design suggests an approach that yields more valid results. This is a combination of the cross-sectional approach and a short-term longitudinal design. In such a design, groups of children of different ages are tested with some overlapping of age intervals. For example, one group of children would be tested at two years of age and again at four years; another group would be tested at four and again at six. Such a study shortens the time required to show patterns of interaction for different ages.

The Ethics of Child Study. Methodological approaches which attempt to study children under controlled circumstances present many ethical dilemmas. Certainly no experiment should be undertaken which would in any way jeopardize a child's health, dignity, or well-being. Both the American Psychological Association (1) and the Society of Research in Child Development (11) have formulated guidelines for investigators to follow in order to promote the highest ethical standards in research with children. Despite the inherent limitations in studying children, many aspects of child psychology can be explored with human subjects through techniques which rely on observation or examination, and even by use of carefully designed experiments which avoid negative effects.

In some instances, animals can be used as substitutes for humans. Although most investigators advise a measure of caution in the generalization of findings obtained from animal studies, the study of animal behavior has frequently led to valid conclusions regarding human behavior. Harlow's studies on infant-mother interactions in monkeys provided greater understanding of the mothering experience and the emotional needs of human babies (7).

2
Principles and Theories of Development

Underlying and giving direction to the study of child psychology are a number of concepts, principles, and theories. Considered together, they provide an appreciation of the dynamics of human development and an understanding of its many facets. This chapter provides an overview of these basic precepts. In later chapters they will be discussed in more detail as they apply to various aspects of growth and development.

PRINCIPLES OF DEVELOPMENT

Psychological development is intrinsically bound to the physical organism and its growth. As an individual grows physically, from conception through the birth process and through the different stages of life, psychological development becomes increasingly important. There is an interweaving of the physical with the psychological; physical growth affecting psychological development, and psychological development in turn affecting physical growth. Although development is intricate, combining the effects of many forces, it is governed by some fundamental principles and proceeds in an orderly way through a series of patterns. Some of the concepts, forces, and governing principles of development are presented in this section.

Maturation. A major concept that explains the orderly change and universal patterns of development is maturation. According to this concept, behaviors and abilities emerge as related physical structures developing according to the innate mechanisms of heredity. Each child is born genetically programed; during the life span, various parts of his organ systems grow and develop at different times. In the earliest stages of life, cell division takes place at an accelerated pace, then slows down and even stops entirely for some organ systems. Specialized cells, such as muscle cells, continue to multiply.

Bone growth, eruption of teeth, and the hormonal changes of adolescence are examples of physical maturation. Examples of early behaviors that unfold are walking, talking, and sphincter control. These milestones in development cannot take place until the muscular and nervous systems have sufficiently matured.

Maturation, although physical in nature, can be facilitated or inhibited by environmental factors. The degree to which life experiences influence maturational development has been a subject of controversy for some time. The extreme positions are, on the one hand, that maturation cannot be accelerated or retarded by environmental influences, and, on the other, that the environment determines the schedule and manner of maturational growth. The centrist position asserts that some biological structures and abilities are primarily, if not exclusively, controlled by maturation while others are more responsive to environmental pressures. Further, it recognizes the interaction of innate and environmental factors in many aspects of development. The degree to which this interaction influences development depends on such considerations as the timing of the environmental event and the value assigned to the behavior in question. Innate musical genius, for example, usually requires environmental encouragement from an early age, as does athletic skill. Thus, the innate maturational schedule sets up biological *readiness* to grow and learn, while environment and experience determine whether the full growth or learning potential of the individual is attained. Nutritional deficiencies may retard maturational forces with regard to growth potentials such as height; anxiety due to unpleasant experiences can interfere with hormone production in adolescence and delay menstruation; and enrichment of experience through verbal and visual stimulation may facilitate and enhance cognitive development.

Continuity and Discontinuity. Although growth proceeds steadily toward maturity of physical structures, it does not do so at an even pace. Periods of rapid growth follow relatively quiet spans of time, a phenomenon known as *discontinuity of growth rate*. During the embryonic and fetal periods of development the baby grows from a single cell to birth size, all within approximately nine months. This relatively quick pace continues during early infancy then decelerates gradually until adolescence, when there is a sudden spurt of growth again.

Asynchronous Growth. Superimposed on this pattern of spurts and lags in general growth rate is the differential growth of various organ systems and body parts. This variation in growth rate and time among body regions is called *asynchronous growth*. At birth the head is much larger in relation to the rest of the body than it is two years later. The trunk, arms, hands, legs, feet, and vital organs such as the heart and lungs take the stage for increased growth at different times while the other body parts and organ systems wait in the wings until it is their turn for accelerated development.

Predictable Patterns of Development. Despite the varying rates of growth and development, the patterns of change are well charted and predictable.

DIFFERENTIATION. The child develops from the simple to the complex in terms of physical and behavioral skills; this is known as the principle of *differentiation*. General responses precede specific ones. The general-to-specific response pattern refers to such instances as a baby's categorization of all furry animals as "doggy" before differentiating particular animals, and, on a motoric level, to the generalized fashion in which hands and fingers are used before the fingers develop refined skills.

GROWTH GRADIENTS. Growth takes place in two general directions: from the center axis outward and from the top down.

The Proximo-Distal Principle. Growth proceeds from the central axis of the body (trunk) to the extremities (hands and feet).

The Cephalo-Caudal Principle. Growth proceeds from head to foot; thus the hands are functional before the feet.

Individual Differences in Development. While the basic principles already described apply to all of human development, there are marked individual differences in the timing, quantity, and quality of that development. Such differences can be noted even before the baby is born; for example, some babies are more active than others during the gestation period. Certainly, individual differences are obvious in newborns, whose weight and body length vary considerably. Babies differ in every possible way, from degree of motor activity to response to environmental stimuli. These differences, attributable to both genetic and prenatal factors, combine with the influences and experiences of life to produce individuals each of whom is unique. Consequently, such progressions as the development and refinement of skills and the unfolding of intellectual and cognitive abilities follow an individual pattern, while at the same time the overall pattern followed by each child is characteristic of all human beings. There are average times at which children begin to walk, talk, become toilet trained, and develop secondary sex characteristics, but no one person conforms to the average in all respects. Each individual follows his own personal timetable within the broad range of the human schedule.

Critical Periods. Critical periods are times of rapid growth for a particular organ system during which it is especially vulnerable to intrusive and harmful influences. During prenatal life, organ systems undergo rapid development in a fixed but overlapping sequence. Rubella (German measles) contracted by the mother in early pregnancy can cause birth defects such as brain damage, heart disease, blindness, deafness, and malformed extremities; the severity of the particular defect depends upon the time of the onset of the illness. Certain drugs (such as thalidomide) ingested by the mother during the first eight weeks of pregnancy also cause severe deformity in the embryo (17).

The concept of critical periods has been extended somewhat cautiously to other times of life. Case histories of institutionalized infants (18) and deprivation studies of animals, such as Harlow's classic studies of monkeys (9), indicate that the first two years of life are a critical period for normal emotional and social development. Emotional neglect over a prolonged period can retard development in all areas, including intellect, language, and personality.

Developmental Tasks. In the 1950s Robert Havighurst applied the idea of critical periods to learning readiness and the many adaptations the child must make at various formative periods (8). According to Havighurst, there are certain periods throughout life during which specific skills must be acquired and particular adjustments must be made. If the child successfully masters the tasks at the appropriate time, that mastery becomes the stepping stone to success in the next period; failure to do so leads to difficulty with succeeding tasks, and to unhappiness and maladjustment. Some of these tasks, such as learning to walk and to talk, are directly related to physical maturation, whereas others, such as learning to read and getting along with age-mates, are based on a combination of influences, tapping physical, cultural, and psychological resources.

The specific developmental tasks necessary for successful life adjustment change from generation to generation. Such skills as academic proficiency and vocational specialization are more indicative of adult success today than they were in the past. Accepting one's physique, preparing for marriage and family life, and achieving a satisfactory psychosexual identification have been complicated by social movements and changing mores and norms. As the traditional definitions of masculinity and femininity in our society have become more fluid, achieving a masculine or feminine social role has become more difficult. Nevertheless, the basic developmental tasks must be mastered.

Imprinting. Imprinting, which is based on the critical-period concept, is the unlearned attachment of some social animals, particularly birds, to the first moving object they encounter immediately after birth. In the usual course of events that object is the mother, but goslings have imprinted to human beings and even to toy figures. Imprinting is limited to a critical period of two or three days after birth; after that, it is no longer possible. The attachment of baby to mother in humans is often cited as a parallel to imprinting. However, the occurrence of imprinting in humans does not lend itself to documentation and therefore remains controversial.

Cultural Determinants. One of the most potent forces defining and giving direction to the growth potential of children is the culture into which they are born. Interestingly, cultural influences are unobtrusive and are generally taken for granted. The needs and expectations for skill development in young children vary tremendously in different cultures. For example, from Margaret Mead's description of life in New Guinea, we learn that the Manus child must literally learn to sink or swim at a very early age because his people live in thatched houses, on stilts, over a wide lagoon with shifting tides (10). Accordingly, by five years of age the Manus child swims well and can even paddle a canoe. In most Western societies a five-year-old is considered too young to perform such skills. Yet investigators have found that children in our society sixteen months of age or younger can be taught to swim and even to roller skate proficiently.

In addition to skill development, each culture defines the distinctive tastes and sex-role attributes of its members. Whale blubber and squid arouse salivation and appetite in youngsters in some parts of the world and revulsion in others. Parents in some cultures reward aggressive behavior; others prize passivity. Varying attitudes toward money, achievement, cleanliness, and other values are acquired by children from the culture in which they live. Standards are transmitted by parents, taught in schools, and learned through observation of adult and peer models who are part of the child's everyday world. Once learned, they are taken for granted.

THE ROLE OF THEORY IN CHILD PSYCHOLOGY

In a beginning course in psychology some student is likely to remark, "Why study psychology? It's all a matter of common sense." When behavioral or other psychological phenomena are carefully examined, however, it is clear that what people do, say, or feel often does not make sense. How does one explain the obsessive need of an individual to wash his hands over and over again? What simple explanation is there for stuttering, or fear of wide open spaces? Many behavioral manifestations cannot readily be explained by "common sense." Theory is the integrated set of propositions or hypotheses formulated to explain complex phenomena, and specifically in child psychology, to make understandable the psychological development of a baby as he grows from a single cell to a complex adult.

Understanding Normal and Abnormal Behavior. Examination of normal behavior leads to a better understanding of abnormal functioning; conversely, the study of abnormal behavior enhances our knowledge of normalcy. For example, we pay little attention to our breathing processes until we, for some reason, experience respiratory difficulty. The same is true of walking, talking, sleeping, learning, and sexual activity. Numerous propositions are advanced to explain the process of normal growth and development. These propositions, or hypotheses, are used as the bases for understanding the abnormal as well as the normal.

Spur to Research. Having formulated and proposed hypotheses, the theorists are then challenged to prove or disprove, support or reject, their conjectured explanations. In this way research tests and explores specific hypotheses. For example, researchers have investigated the validity of theories dealing with the relationship between infant stimulation and later intellectual development and the correlation between early maternal deprivation and personality deficits. The findings derived from such studies have enriched our knowledge of child growth and development. New psychological insights have brought about changes in obstetrical and hospital procedures relative to infant care, revisions in educational curricula, and new approaches in child-rearing practices.

Preventive Mental Hygiene. Research findings in child psychology enable us to produce environments which facilitate the development of happy rather than unhappy children and adults. Through preventive mental-hygiene measures, psychological damage to children can be averted or minimized and obstacles to a happy and productive life may at least be partially overcome.

Aid to the Psychologically Maladjusted. Numerous therapeutic interventions have evolved as a result of research into the causes of psychological deviancy. Tranquilizers and other medications have given new hope to many institutionalized patients. Individual and group psychotherapy, behavior modification, hypnotherapy, rational therapy, and gestalt therapy are all methods of treatment which derive from and are based on theories of personality development. As further study is made of the validity of these theories, treatment techniques and approaches will correspondingly be improved, modified, or even discontinued.

THEORIES OF DEVELOPMENT

Child psychology has progressed far beyond the untested observations and speculations of the early contributors to the field. Many theories have been advanced to explain and predict psychological phenomena. Some of these are broad in scope, attempting to comprehend the lifelong experience of the individual, whereas others focus on specific aspects of human behavior and learning.

Classification of theoretical orientations in child psychology may be made in a variety of ways. Here they are grouped into two major categories: learning theories and stage theories. There are also many conceptualizations that overlap these categories or combine aspects of one or more of them; such cross-categorical groupings are those focusing on the sociological, cultural, and humanistic forces in child development.

Learning Theories. Learning theories are based on the assumption that all behavior, with the exception of some basic reflexes, is learned through the associational connection of stimulus and response (S-R). Although these theories concede that genetic endowment and maturational growth play some part in behavioral development, they stress the role of the environment and experience.

CLASSICAL CONDITIONING: PAVLOV. In the early 1900s a Russian psychologist, Ivan Pavlov, experimenting with dogs in his laboratory, discovered that the animals made an association between the keeper and the food he brought, and salivated at the mere sight of the keeper (11). It was not necessary for the dogs to first see, smell, or taste the food; they only had to see the person who usually presented it. In classical conditioning terms, the natural or unconditioned stimulus, food, produced the unconditioned response, salivation, which is a reflexive response. When the association between the keeper and food was established the keeper became the substitute or conditioned stimulus in eliciting the reflexive unconditioned response, salivation, which then became a learned, conditioned response. Pavlov carried his work further by conditioning the dogs to salivate at the sound of a bell rung just prior to the presentation of food. The learning or conditioning became so strong after a time that the dogs salivated at the sound of the bell. This discovery became the foundation for what was to become the behaviorist movement in psychology, led by John B. Watson.

Clark L. Hull, Kenneth Spence, and Edward Thorndike expanded

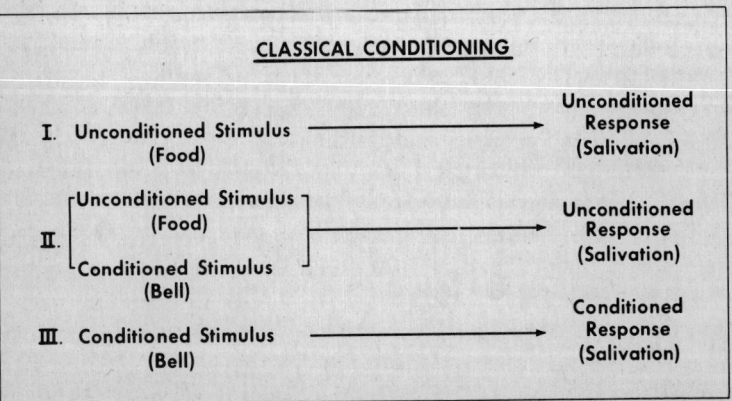

classical conditioning theory to account for conceptual and incidental learning. Thorndike's work with instrumental learning was a precursor to B. F. Skinner's theory of operant conditioning (1).

OPERANT CONDITIONING: SKINNER. In classical conditioning, the behavior, the unconditioned response, is a natural reflexive reaction such as salivation, sucking movements, and some kinds of fear responses in infants. In operant conditioning, developed by B. F. Skinner in the 1930s, the behavior is not elicited by an unconditioned stimulus but is emitted spontaneously, then reinforced (16).

Operant conditioning is derived from Thorndike's law of effect, which states that satisfactorily rewarded behavior will be repeated under like conditions. Skinner's work went well beyond that of Thorndike. Working with more complex behaviors in birds and animals than had his predecessors, Skinner extended the concept of operant conditioning to human learning. He demonstrated that desired behavior could be elicited by rewarding that behavior at the moment it occurred, thus reinforcing the desired response. A teacher could modify an unruly child's behavior by immediately rewarding any slight improvement in conduct. If the child verbalized angry feelings instead of acting out aggressively, he would be rewarded. Through a program of reinforcement, the undesirable behavior would in time be replaced by the more socially acceptable one. According to Skinner, almost all behavior can be shaped or modified by careful provision of reinforcements which encourage the individual to operate actively upon his environment to obtain a reward. Skinner terms this operant (as opposed to respondent) learning, or conditioning. It is also known as instrumental learning.

The principles of operant conditioning have been utilized in the development of teaching machines used for programed learning. They are also the basis of behavior modification techniques for correcting maladaptive habits such as stuttering, bed-wetting, and nail-biting.

SOCIAL LEARNING THEORY. Robert Sears and his colleagues, working within the framework of S-R (stimulus-response) theory, constructed an approach to learning that owes much to concepts derived from psychoanalysis and anthropology (14). Sears, along with Neal Miller, John Dollard, Albert Bandura (15), and others, used the psychoanalytic concept of identification, interweaving it with the dependency needs of children and stimulus-response reinforcement. Social learning theory provides that children learn by observation of role models and by the reinforcement received when they imitate admired models. Thus, boys observing and identifying with fathers will be rewarded by attention, love, and approval when they follow or imitate their father-models.

Observation, identification, imitation, modeling, and reinforcement are essential features of social learning theory, although their relative importance is a matter upon which some investigators disagree. Bandura and his colleagues, who have conducted extensive studies in this area, point out that the observation of prestigious models in and of itself can stimulate imitation even in the absence of reinforcement. Thus a child might imitate the behavior of an admired athlete although no direct reward is forthcoming (2,3).

Stage Theories. Stage theories view development as a progressive unfolding of the physiologically based characteristics of the child. Thus the physical stages of development and the maturational process are of primary interest in stage theory. All aspects of behavior—intellectual, emotional, social, and psychological—are considered to be linked to physical maturation. Stage theory assumes discontinuity of growth; each stage involves a change in form and organization of behavior, but incorporates elements of the stage preceding it.

MATURATION THEORY: GESELL. Arnold Gesell is probably the best-known of the early stage theorists. Although Gesell studied developmental psychology under G. Stanley Hall at Clark University, his subsequent work was in large part influenced by his medical training and his observation of infant behavior at the Gesell Institute of Child Development at Yale University. Gesell saw maturation as the essential factor in development. He and his colleagues Francis Ilg and Louise Ames devised schedules of child development in the major areas of behavior: motor, adaptive, language, and personal-social (6,7). The behavior norms for each age level were based on physical maturation. Though he acknowledged the possibility of some environmental influence on genetically programed characteristics, Gesell remained steadfast in his position that development progresses inexorably through a series of specified stages from infancy to adulthood.

COGNITIVE STAGE THEORY: PIAGET. Jean Piaget, a Swiss psychologist and the foremost exponent of cognitive development theory, proposed that the growth and development of cognition in children follows a systematic and sequential pattern (12). Starting at birth, each child passes through discrete, progressively more sophisticated stages of cognitive development, each of which enables him to adapt more effectively to his environment.

Piaget's stages of cognitive development are the sensorimotor stage, the preoperational stage, the stage of concrete operations, and the stage of formal operations (13).

The Sensorimotor Stage (birth to eighteen months). This stage is characterized by an acquisition of motor skills, adaptive behavior, and the intake of information at the most elementary level.

The Preoperational Stage (eighteen months to age seven). At this stage, children learn to adapt more directly and actively to their environment. Motor skills are extended and refined, and language skills are developed. At the outset of this stage, children perceive meanings in terms of their own unique experiences (egocentrism) and only toward the end are they able to appreciate the ideas of others (socialized thought) and gain a wider perspective. They are moving toward a higher level of conceptual thought. The child cannot generalize adequately yet; his logic is likely to be faulty.

The Stage of Concrete Operations (age seven to twelve). In this third stage the child begins to show greater ability to reason and think objectively. He can understand that quantity remains constant even if shape changes (conservation). He can keep in mind more than one property of an object and, therefore, is able to sort objects according to both shape and color (classification). He can add and subtract (reversibility). Understanding of relationships between categories of things increases, but it is difficult to look ahead, to anticipate and plan. As the title of this stage indicates, children of this period can perform many mental operations as long as they deal with concrete, here-and-now activities. They cannot readily generalize or think in abstractions.

The Stage of Formal Operations (age twelve onward). Here the child moves into the highest stage of cognitive development. He becomes increasingly capable of abstract thinking and is able to form hypotheses and test them by logical reasoning. He can experiment with cause-and-effect relationships on a higher level than previously. As the child becomes less self-centered and better able to handle abstraction, he develops the ability to make moral judgments. No longer is he tied to absolute codes of morality (moral realism); he can be flexible and interpret issues according to the circumstances (moral relativism).

Piagetian theory proposes that children learn at their own pace, although the mechanisms for learning can be, and perhaps should be, provided by the environment. These mechanisms include the development of schemata, the motor and cognitive patterns of behavior which the child acquires as he responds to the stimuli he encounters in life. Learning and cognitive development take place as new experiences are incorporated into schemata previously developed, thus enlarging and enriching the child's repertoire of acts and ideas. The steps through which these adaptive processes take place include *assimilation, accommodation,* and *equilibration.* A new object or experience is assimilated by the child into existing schemata. A baby given a new toy will play with that toy in the same way he played with all previous ones. As he discovers new properties of the toy, he will begin to change his pattern of action with regard to it. He will ring a bell, for instance, by deliberately shaking it, or will squeeze a rubber doll to obtain a squeak. This mechanism, called accommodation, expands the child's schemata to include the new toy. Accommodation involves the modification of existing responses to include a set of new responses which embrace the properties, quality, and requirements of the new experience, be it toy or idea.

As the process of assimilation and accommodation becomes stabilized, the child moves adaptively toward intellectual maturity. His schemata become more flexible and more responsive to the increasing array of life experiences. As this balance of old and new achieves a higher level of adaptation, equilibrium is said to have been achieved.

PSYCHOANALYTIC THEORY: FREUD, ERIKSON. Freud, like Piaget, proposed a theory of development based on a series of distinct stages (5). His approach and concerns, however, were very different. Whereas Piaget restricted his study of development to cognition, Freud sought to explain the entire range of human behavior in terms of psychosexual and personality development. Freud's stages of development were based on zones of the body, Piaget's on ways of thinking. The child's satisfactory progression through the various stages was, for Freud, far from assured. He saw the path of normal growth subject to roadblocks in the form of inappropriate experiences. Freud's theories developed from clinical practice rather than laboratory studies. Trained as a physician, he worked with emotionally disturbed patients, using hypnosis at first, and later shifting to free association.

The Libido; Cathexis. In Freud's view, the individual is motivated by biologically based, instinctual drives, that are categorized as sexual, hostile-aggressive, and self-preservative. Freud's conception of sexuality was much broader than the commonly accepted definition, and included a wide spectrum of pleasurable sensations. The instinctual drives are expressed through a system of psychic energy of which each person is born with a fixed amount. Freud called this sexual energy the *libido*. As a need arises within the individual, energy is excited and a drive or motivation is set in motion. As a result, the excitation is reduced and the need fulfilled. Depending on which need is activated, the libido is directed toward sources required to satisfy the particular need. These sources may be food, people, ideas, or even parts of the individual's own body. Gratification is obtained through the process of *cathexis,* which is the attachment of the libidinal energy onto the particular source. Behavior is thus regarded as a series of needs and urges that activate the libido, which then causes the individual to act, think, or feel. An essential element in this aspect of Freudian theory is its dynamic nature. The human personality is conceived to be in a constant state of action and reaction, a process both initiated and responded to by internal and external forces.

The Unconscious. Foremost among psychoanalytic concepts is that of the unconscious, the reservoir of memories, wishes, impulses, and feelings that are threatening or not in keeping with the individual's value system. The unconscious also contains a variety of personal perceptions or ideas that have been rejected for one reason or another. The unconscious, however, is not simply a repository of forgotten or sleeping memories and wishes. It is an active agent, initiating, inhibiting, or shaping behavior.

The individual functions simultaneously on three levels of consciousness, which are (1) *the conscious* level of mental and personality functioning in which the person knows the content and roots of his thinking and behavior, (2) *the preconscious,* sometimes called the subconscious, the level just below the surface of consciousness, which may be brought to awareness under certain conditions, and (3) *the unconscious,* the deepest level, wherein thoughts, feelings, or impulses are actively kept out of either preconscious or conscious levels of functioning.

The Three Structures of Personality. Freud recognized three divisions of the personality: the *id, ego,* and *superego.* The id, the oldest structure, "contains everything that is inherited, that is present at birth, that is fixed in the constitution—above all, therefore, the instincts . . ." (5, p. 14). The id is nonrational and impulse-oriented. Gratification and reduction of excitation are its goals, and it is driven by the *pleasure principle.* The ego arises out of the id and serves as a mediator between the impulsive wishes of the id and reality. In its role as a preserver of the organism, the ego sees that appropriate needs are satisfied adequately and safely. It must thus come to know, remember, and accurately evaluate experiences encountered throughout life. The ego is driven by the *reality principle,* which supersedes the pleasure principle as the personality matures. The superego develops in early childhood and acts as the internalized voice of the parent. It is what is more commonly called the conscience: the pool of values and judgments of right and wrong. The superego serves as a guard over the ego, ensuring that the individual's moral values have not been violated in the ego's drive to satisfy needs and wishes.

Defense Mechanisms. Freud describes various defense mechanisms which are used by the ego as unconscious means of avoiding anxiety and resolving conflicts when more direct approaches are unsuccessful. The following are some of the more important defense mechanisms:

1. *Repression* is the pushing of disturbing thoughts or feelings from consciousness into the unconscious. All defense mechanisms to some extent depend upon repression.

2. *Denial* serves to prevent an unwelcome idea, feeling, or perception from entering into awareness. In this way reality becomes distorted. For example, the student does not see the homework assignment on the blackboard, and the child viewing television does not hear his mother calling him to dinner.

3. *Rationalization* allows the individual to justify his actions by resorting to self-deception. The child actually believes that the reading test he failed was unfair, or that the teacher is unsympathetic.

4. *Projection* is the defensive tactic by which the person sees in others qualities and characteristics which he himself possesses but does not wish to acknowledge. The rejected characteristic is projected

onto someone else. The young girl who accuses a friend of being a "flirt" really doesn't see herself in this role.

5. *Displacement* enables individuals to shift unacceptable feelings from one object or person to a safer one. For example, it is more acceptable to kick a chair than a younger brother, or it may be more advantageous to vent one's hostility on a teacher than on a parent.

The defense mechanisms already described are but a few of the many utilized by the ego. They are sometimes called behavior or adjustment mechanisms. Other defense mechanisms include *withdrawal, sublimation, compensation, reaction formation,* and *intellectualization.*

Freud's Stages of Development. Freud's emphasis on sexuality as a force in development is evident in his designation of personality development in terms of psychosexual stages.

1. The Oral Stage. In infancy, the mouth is the center of satisfaction. Nursing not only serves physical needs but also provides gratification from sucking and associated pleasant sensations. Besides sucking, the mouth is used to examine objects, and later for eating and biting.

2. The Anal Stage. In toddlerhood, the focus of attention shifts to the anal area. The child is gaining control over the sphincter muscles and derives pleasure from withholding and expelling feces. Because toilet training takes place at this period, it may be a time of frustration and conflict between parent and child.

3. The Phallic Stage. When children are about four years of age, their interest centers on the genital areas. At this time, an awareness of the anatomical differences between the sexes occurs. There is an increase in masturbatory activity and use of words related to sex and bodily functions. The strong attachment of the boy to his mother generates intense feelings of frustration and resentment known as the *Oedipus complex.* The young son wishes to displace his father in his mother's affection, but is afraid that his father will discover secret feelings and punish him with castration. In order to resolve his Oedipal conflict and relieve his *castration anxiety* the son relinquishes his mother as a sexualized love object and eventually seeks a substitute in another woman as a mate. In the process, he develops a further *identification* with his father, who becomes a model of

maleness rather than a hated rival. The young girl goes through an analogous experience (*Electra complex*) characterized by penis envy, eventually resolved by her identification with her mother.

4. Latency. At about six years of age, when the child enters school, a period of sexual quiescence begins. Lessening concerns with sexual conflicts and the anxieties of the previous stages permit the child to devote his energies to cognitive learning during the next six years.

5. The Genital Stage. At adolescence, the young person approaches sexual maturity, physically, socially, and psychologically. During this stage he may relive some of the earlier conflicts. Homosexual attachments may develop, but sexual interest usually turns toward the opposite sex.

Psychoanalytic theory recognizes that the growing child may be confronted with many obstacles as he progresses through the various stages of development, interferences that may thwart healthy emotional growth. If severe trauma is suffered during one of the psychosexual stages, the child may become *fixated* or bound to some elements of that stage. In later life, he may then *regress* to the immature behavior characteristic of the stage in which fixation occurred. For example, fixation at the oral stage may result in a tendency to overeat during periods of anxiety.

Although Freud was the pioneer in psychoanalytic theory, others who followed him have added to and modified portions or all of his ideas. Carl Jung, Alfred Adler, Harry Stack Sullivan, Karen Horney, Erich Fromm, and Erik Erikson are a few who have played important roles in the psychoanalytic movement. Of this group, we shall limit ourselves to a brief description of some of the views of Erik Erikson.

ERIKSON'S PSYCHOSOCIAL STAGES. Erikson expanded psychoanalytic theory to include a social dimension (4). The first five of Erikson's eight stages of development parallel Freud's stages, but are psychosocial rather than psychosexual. The three additional stages pertain to the psychosocial adjustments of adulthood. During each of the eight stages, the individual must resolve the developmental crises that characterize it before he can move on successfully to the next stage. The eight stages proposed by Erikson are as follows:

1. Birth to one year: trust vs. mistrust
2. Two to three years: autonomy vs. doubt

3. Four to five years: initiative vs. guilt
4. Six to eleven years: industry vs. inferiority
5. Twelve to eighteen years: identity vs. role confusion
6. Young adulthood: intimacy vs. isolation
7. Middle age: generativity vs. self-absorption
8. Old age: integrity vs. despair

A number of theoretical concepts have been described in this chapter; there are of course others which have not been discussed. These include Kurt Lewin's field theory, the humanistic or third-force psychology of Abraham Maslow, the various phenomenological and existential theories, and the nondirective approach of Carl Rogers.

3

Life Begins: Prenatal and Neonatal Development

Although birth is the dramatic emergence of the new individual into the world, the actual beginning of life precedes it by approximately nine months. At that time two cells come together, a union that initiates a complex process of cell division and differentiation that results in a functioning human being capable of living outside the womb. During the interval between conception and birth, many factors affect the way the unborn child develops; indeed, there are influences at work even before the moment of conception. This chapter will examine some of these factors and trace development from the period immediately prior to the union of the sperm and ovum through birth and the early weeks of postnatal life.

PRENATAL DEVELOPMENT

A variety of genetic and environmental factors are operative during the period prior to birth.

Genetic Influences. Crucial variables in development arise from the very nature of the genes entering into the union of cells at the time of conception. Since conception involves the union of a reproductive cell from the mother and a reproductive cell from the father, the resulting cell contains chromosomes and genes from both parents, with all the characteristics inherent in these genes.

CHROMOSOMES. Chromosomes are the rod-shaped bodies present in the nucleus of each cell. They are the carriers of the genes. In the process of *mitosis,* each cell divides so that the two resulting cells receive identical chromosomes. This is possible because the chromosomes have duplicated themselves. Thus, as the child grows, each cell in his body contains the same chromosomes, and thus the same genes.

GENES. Genes are the transmitters of heredity traits and characteristics. The long strands of DNA (deoxyribonucleic acid) of which they are composed carry the genetic code. The instructions in this code order the production of particular enzymes and other proteins that direct the activities of the cell. Thus the genes carry the information that directs biological growth and development. There are genes that determine characteristics common to the species (humans are distinguished from apes by traits such as bipedalism and hairlessness) as well as characteristics specific to the individual (color of eyes, skin pigmentation, height potential, and the like).

Recombinant DNA technology (gene-splicing), which involves the transplantation of a segment of genetic material from a cell of one species to a cell of another, has been the subject of much controversy in recent years. While alteration of the genes can lead to a better understanding of the fundamentals of life and thus extend medical and other knowledge, some scientists are concerned that genetic engineering can also pose ecological and biological hazards. Extensive governmental guidelines regulating DNA experimentation are therefore being developed to ensure the safety of such research.

GAMETES. The living organism is composed of trillions of cells, all of which contain 46 chromosomes, in 23 pairs. There are two kinds of cells, body cells and germ cells. As stated above, body cells divide by mitosis, each of the two resulting cells receiving a full set of chromosomes. The germ cells give rise to the reproductive cells, called gametes, through a process called *meiosis*. In meiosis, the germ cells divide in such a way that the number of chromosomes in each of the resulting cells is 23, half the number in the body cells. When the male gamete, or sperm, penetrates the female gamete, or ovum, the new cell, called a zygote, contains the chromosomes of both parents, 23 from each.

Each gamete contains one of a pair of chromosomes known as sex chromosomes. These special chromosomes, which under a microscope resemble an X and a Y, are responsible for sex determination. An ovum has only an X chromosome, whereas a sperm cell contains either an X or a Y chromosome. When a sperm cell with an X chromosome fertilizes an ovum, a girl is produced. If, however, the sperm carries a Y chromosome, the baby will be a boy. In recent years, some research has been directed toward developing techniques for preselection of the sex of the child (2). Some of the methods now being utilized for sex-choice determination involve artificial insemination of a Y chromosome, timing of ovulation, and amniocentesis. The latter method, which involves analysis of a small sample of amniotic fluid, is primarily used to detect genetic abnormalities (i.e., Down's syndrome and Tay-Sach's disease) rather than to control the sex of the child. Should these relatively new techniques ever be used for sex-control purposes on a wide scale, it may upset the male-female balance, since polls show a preference for male over female children, especially for a first child.

GREGOR MENDEL AND THE PRINCIPLES OF HEREDITY. In the late nineteenth century, through breeding and crossbreeding of plants, Mendel discovered that certain characteristics are transmitted to the next generation whereas others are not. Further experimentation revealed that the traits apparently not transmitted are, in fact, passed on, but they give way to the dominance of other traits and therefore are not expressed. Mendel proposed that many characteristics of an organism are controlled by a pair of factors, one from each parent, and that one is *dominant* and will be expressed, and the other is *recessive* and will not appear. These factors are now called genes. Thus, a child inheriting a gene for brown eyes from one parent and a gene for blue eyes from the other parent will be brown-eyed because the gene for brown eyes is dominant, while the gene for blue eyes is recessive. If two like genes are inherited, however, that single characteristic will be expressed. A child inheriting blue-eye genes from both parents will have blue eyes. Mendel's laws have led to much research in genetic transmission and have helped to explain the diversity of characteristics evident in different children of the same parents.

THE NATURE-NURTURE CONTROVERSY. The relative importance of heredity and environment in determining human development is a subject of constant debate. Quite obviously, valid answers to the question of which of these forces exerts the greater influence have practical as well as scientific ramifications. Yet, it is extremely difficult, if not impossible, to disentangle the threads of heredity and environment because the two influences interact continuously on development, almost from the moment of conception. There are, nevertheless, certain traits that appear to be related more to genetic than to environmental factors. Among these are such physical characteristics as eye color, some aspects of bone structure, and red-green color blindness. Height is related to gene transmission, although it is certainly influenced by environmental factors such as diet.

Many physical abnormalities are genetically determined. These include hemophilia, sickle-cell anemia, diabetes mellitus, phenylketonuria (PKU), and Down's syndrome.

INTELLIGENCE. The extent to which heredity determines intellectual ability is a particularly controversial issue in the nature-nurture debate. Studies support both environmentalist and hereditarian positions (5). Research with identical and fraternal twins reared apart and together, and with children growing up in biological and in foster homes, yields consistent findings. With respect to IQ, children are found to resemble their biological families more closely than they resemble their foster families. Identical twins reared together show a higher correlation in intelligence than identical twins reared apart. Nevertheless, the IQs of identical twins show a higher correlation coefficient than do those of fraternal twins or siblings. All of these correlations are closer than those of unrelated children. When individual cases in these studies were examined, however, some twins reared apart were found to have marked differences in IQ. Thus the hereditarians and the environmentalists have interpreted the same findings as supporting their divergent positions in the controversy.

Despite the strong stands taken by some proponents of each point of view, most authorities agree that both heredity and environment play significant roles in the development and manifestation of intelligence. Each child is born with a genetically determined constitution which includes the central nervous system. All biological systems, however, are influenced from the moment of conception by the environment in which the initial cell begins its series of divisions. Environmental influences on the baby in utero, such as poor diet, drug ingestion, and infectious diseases of the mother, may damage brain tissues and thus reduce intellectual functioning. After the baby is born, environmental influences increase manyfold. The baby may be born into a family environment that is stimulating and enriching and encourages learning or, alternatively, into an environment that, because of economic, cultural, or other factors, is intellectually limiting and lacking in opportunities for optimum development of intellectual potential. This interplay between the individual's inherent qualities and the influences of his environment goes on constantly from conception to death.

Periodically, the nature-nurture issue becomes a public one. Arguments arise over the funding of special educational programs or the validity of certain remedial or rehabilitative programs. Some academicians, Arthur Jensen (7), for example, question the ability of compensatory education to overcome intellectual deficiencies; they believe that heredity is the major factor in intelligence. Others take the position that life situations are crucial elements in developing intelligence. At present, most psychologists agree that both heredity and environment are important in the development of intelligence, although the relative contribution of each influence is open to question.

PERSONALITY. Another disputed issue in the nature-nurture debate is whether personality traits are transmitted or acquired (16). Many studies give support to the inheritability of certain personality characteristics. Researchers have found, for example, that identical twins are more alike in such qualities as sociability, timidity, and inhibition than are sets of fraternal twins. Other personality traits which have been found to be under some degree of genetic control are depressive tendencies, demonstrativeness, social smiling, and activity levels. The very fact that marked differences in personality traits can be observed in newborn babies is persuasive evidence that these differences are genetic in origin. However, animal and human studies cited in support of a genetic or constitutional component in personality are not universally accepted as clear proof of that position. Some theorists point to the difficulty of isolating any single quality of personality upon which environmental factors are not intimately and constantly acting. It is almost impossible, they say, to trace a multidimensional characteristic to heredity alone when so many nongenetic forces are influencing that characteristic.

Some inherited traits facilitate or impede social acceptance and thereby influence personality development. For example, an extremely short boy or a very tall, thin girl will receive different responses from parents, teachers, and peers than will a tall boy or a well-built girl of moderate height. The particular responses will affect the self-concepts of these youngsters and thus will influence their personality development. These influences, however, cannot be reliably predicted and thus cannot be directly ascribed to heredity.

Although it is hard to prove that complex personality patterns are genetically determined, there is substantial evidence that specific aspects of temperament are inherited. Stella Chess identified nine criteria to differentiate temperamental styles in neonates (1). Differences in patterns of behavior related to activity level, quality of mood, degree of regularity of bodily functions (eating, sleeping, elimination), intensity of reaction, adaptability, distractability, response to new stimuli, intensity of reaction, and attention span and persistence are quite evident at birth, according to Chess. This kind of individuality, present at birth, plays a significant role in the interaction between the child and his environment.

GENETIC DISEASES AND DISORDERS. It is sometimes difficult to isolate specific causes of developmental irregularities and abnormalities. This is particularly true with regard to defects in the child that may be due to gene or chromosomal transmission. There are certain abnormalities, however, the causes of which are known (10).

Down's Syndrome. Babies born with Down's syndrome show severe physical and mental defects. They have been called mongoloid because a tissue formation over the eyelids gives them an Oriental appearance. This disorder has been traced to the abnormal division of one of the chromosomes of chromosomal pair 21, which produces an extra chromosome. The cause of this irregularity is not clear, but the syndrome occurs more frequently in the children of older women.

Sex Chromosomal Deviations. Missing or extra sex chromosomes cause distinct developmental disorders. One of these, *Turner's syndrome,* is due to the presence of only one sex chromosome, the X chromosome, instead of XX (female) or XY (male). This deficiency leads to the birth of an unusually short female child who does not develop normal feminine sex characteristics. In another chromosomal disorder, this one affecting male births, an extra X chromosome is present (XXY). This condition, known as *Klinefelter's syndrome,* is similar to Turner's syndrome in that the child lacks sexual differentiation. Males with this disorder are sterile and have unusual breast development.

Phenylketonuria (PKU). This disorder is caused by a recessive gene which, when present as a pair, prevents the body from breaking down and metabolizing the amino acid called phenylalanine, which is present in milk and most other protein foods. Phenylalanine then

PRENATAL STAGES OF DEVELOPMENT

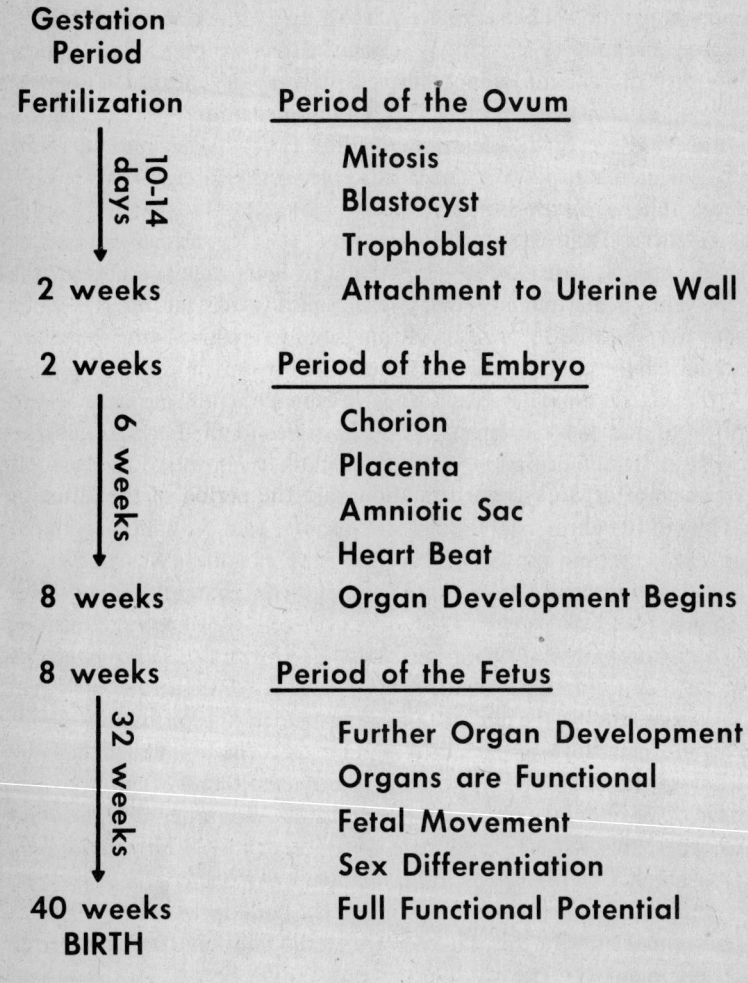

accumulates in the body and damages brain tissues. Fortunately, the presence of this abnormality can be detected early, and phenylalanine can be withheld from the diet. Prenatal diagnostic procedures such as amniocentesis and the Alpha Fetal Protein test (AFP) are now being administered by doctors to detect genetic abnormalities during the early months of pregnancy.

Prenatal Influences. As previously stated, human life begins at the moment of conception. At that time the reproductive cell of the father (sperm) penetrates the wall of the reproductive cell of the mother (ovum). The fertilized ovum, called the zygote, now contains the full complement of chromosomes: 46. From this single cell the new individual will develop. The time from conception to birth is approximately nine calendar months or ten lunar months (28-day cycles). The stages of development during this period and some of the environmental factors that influence prenatal development will be discussed in this section.

STAGES OF DEVELOPMENT. Development from conception to birth, the gestation period, is usually divided into three stages: the period of the ovum, or stage of cell division; the period of the embryo, or stage of organ system formation; and the period of the fetus, or stage of growth.

Period of the Ovum. The first period of gestation lasts about two weeks. Immediately after fertilization, cell division (mitosis) begins. The zygote divides, and the resulting cells continue to divide, forming a hollow sphere called the *blastocyst.* The blastocyst is composed of a group of outer cells, the *trophoblast,* and an inner group of cells that will eventually form the embryo. As the blastocyst is forming, it is floating freely in the uterus. In about two weeks it becomes attached to the uterine wall, which has been prepared to receive it.

Period of the Embryo. This period starts during the second week after fertilization and continues for approximately six weeks. The trophoblast, or outer layer of the blastocyst, becomes the *chorion,* a protective membrane that, along with uterine tissues, forms the placenta. From the placenta, through the umbilical cord, the necessary life-supporting supplies are filtered to the embryo without directly mixing with the mother's blood. The inner cell mass of the blastocyst differentiates into the embryo and the *amniotic* sac. This fluid-filled sac surrounds the embryo and serves a cushioning function.

During the embryonic stage the heart starts to beat, arms, legs, fingers, and toes make their appearance, internal organs begin to form, and the nervous system develops. It is therefore a critical period for the growing organism. Many environmental forces may affect the pregnant woman and in turn harm the embryo. Drug ingestion, radiation, physical injury, and maternal illness all threaten the life of the embryo and its development. Some abnormalities stemming from the gestation period will be discussed in a later section of this chapter.

Period of the Fetus. The fetal stage of prenatal growth starts approximately at the beginning of the third month of pregnancy. The primitive organs and other body structures that made their appearance during the embryo stage continue to form and develop, and gradually become more functional. Movement of the fetus can be felt by the mother at this time. Sex differentiation becomes evident with the development of sex organs and the reproductive systems. At approximately seven months of prenatal age, the fetus becomes capable of independent existence. Although a prematurely born baby of this age requires a great deal of help (much more than one born at full term) in order to survive, nevertheless, all of his life systems are either already functioning in a rudimentary form, or they are ready to function without complete dependence on the mother's body.

Thus, the stage of fetal development prepares the maturing new organism to function with sufficient ability to sustain life after birth. At the end of this period the fetus will emerge from the mother's body, a newborn baby.

ENVIRONMENTAL INFLUENCES ON PRENATAL DEVELOPMENT. From the moment of conception until birth, the unborn child is relatively vulnerable. Many complex and interrelated processes in the mother's body and many forces in the environment may divert development from its normal pattern.

Maternal Age. Prenatal difficulties increase with the mother's age, probably because of hormonal changes. There is a greater chance of mentally retarded offspring, miscarriage, stillbirth, and neonatal death among mothers over thirty-five than among younger mothers. However, statistics also show a high mortality rate for infants of teen-age mothers.

Maternal Nutrition. During prenatal life, dietary deficiencies can prevent the fullest growth of the various body systems. Undernourishment may, for example, impede brain cell development. Recently, nutritional research has repudiated the myth that the body of the mother nourishes the prenatal organism prior to taking its own nourishment (11). The baby's needs are more likely to be met after the needs of the mother's own body have been fulfilled. A complete and adequate maternal diet is therefore especially necessary to ensure the health and normal development of the baby.

Maternal Emotional State. Endocrine secretions and blood chemistry change markedly when a person is under intense emotional stress. Therefore, hormones and chemicals in the bloodstream of the mother who is experiencing anxiety, tension, or fear can be transmitted through the placenta and affect the baby. If such changes occur at critical periods of organ formation, the baby may suffer harmful consequences, particularly if the emotional stress is of long duration. One study reports an increase in fetal activity during periods of maternal stress, and another links colic (a crying reaction to physical distress) during early infancy with maternal tension during pregnancy (12). Despite these findings, there is no conclusive proof that maternal emotional states have adverse effects on prenatal development. It is difficult to separate prenatal influences from those of the postnatal period. Women who are tense during pregnancy are likely to be tense after the baby is born.

Drugs and Toxic Agents. Drugs in the mother's blood also enter the fetal bloodstream and may have adverse effects on the well-being and development of the unborn child. The results can be tragic, as in the case of thalidomide, a drug once prescribed for pregnant women to relieve nausea. Women who took this drug during the first three months of their pregnancy gave birth to seriously deformed babies. Findings on the effect of such psychoactive drugs as LSD and heroin on prenatal development are inconclusive. There is evidence, however, that pain-relieving drugs administered prior to delivery can affect the newborn for some time after birth (3). Whether such effects, revealed by a lessening of attentiveness, are symptomatic of deeper physiological damage is not known. Pregnant women are cautioned to take drugs only when prescribed by a physician, and to avoid commonly used drugs and medications sold over the counter.

Alcohol. Babies of alcoholic mothers exposed to alcohol in utero can suffer growth deficiencies, malformations, and varying degrees of mental retardation. Even mild social drinking is being discouraged during pregnancy because of the harmful effects of alcohol on the developing fetus. According to the National Institute of Alcohol Abuse and Alcoholism, a division of the U.S. Department of H.E.W., two drinks of hard liquor taken daily by a pregnant woman could endanger the fetus. Birth deformities attributable to fetal alcohol syndrome include congenital eye and ear defects, heart abnormalities, and extra digits.

Tobacco. Establishing a direct relationship between the use of a specific substance by the pregnant woman and developmental disorders in the baby is particularly difficult in the case of smoking because many variables must be considered in measuring the level of tobacco use. The kinds of tobacco, their tar content, the amount of tobacco consumed, and the extent to which smoke is inhaled, all must be taken into account. There are indications, nevertheless, that women who are heavy smokers during pregnancy have a greater chance of having premature babies than do women who abstain. Moreover, full-term babies born to mothers who smoke weigh less on the average than babies born to nonsmokers (17).

Maternal Disease and Illness. Certain infectious diseases contracted by the expectant mother can affect the embryo and fetus. If rubella (German measles) develops during the first trimester of pregnancy, in all likelihood the baby will be born with abnormalities such as deafness, blindness, and mental deficiency. Syphilis, gonorrhea, mumps, influenza, and polio may also harm the developing organism.

Diabetes may cause damage to the bones, tissues, or organs of the fetus. Toxemia, a disorder of pregnancy in which the mother develops blood poisoning, can produce congenital defects and the baby may be born prematurely.

Radiation. With the discovery that radiation can damage human tissue, the potential hazard of X-ray exposure to the unborn child was immediately recognized. Both physical and mental disturbances and abnormalities in babies have been traced to large doses of radiation sustained prior to birth. Although small doses of radiation may not be dangerous, the build-up of X-ray irradiation over a period of time presents a risk to both mother and child.

Rh Incompatibility. When the mother's blood is Rh negative and the blood of the fetus is Rh positive, antibodies produced in the mother destroy the fetal red blood cells. The result is anemia and oxygen deficiency that may lead to termination of the pregnancy or death of the baby shortly after birth. Rh factor incompatibility can be determined by blood tests, and appropriate measures can be taken during pregnancy or immediately after the baby is born to avoid serious consequences. First-born children are rarely affected by Rh incompatibility.

BIRTH

The period of prenatal development is one of remarkable growth from a single cell to an organism which is ready for independent life.

The Birth Process. Toward the end of the ninth month of pregnancy, the fetus shifts its position in the womb so that its head is pointed downward, and settles lower in the uterine cavity. As the time of birth approaches, uterine contractions, or labor pains, begin, and the vaginal opening dilates. The mother may help the baby's passage through the birth canal by bearing down with her abdominal muscles. When the actual birth takes place, the mother may be given anesthesia. The baby's head emerges, unless it is a breech birth (buttocks first). The umbilical cord is then tied and severed, separating the baby from its mother. The baby's physical status is then assessed according to the Apgar score, which is a set of guides for rating breathing, heart rate, muscle tone, reflexes, and color. Soon after the birth, the placenta is expelled.

"Natural" Childbirth. Some parents prefer a birth process that avoids the use of medication or anesthesia. The method referred to as natural childbirth originated with a London physician, Grantly Dick-Read, who noticed that some women did not experience pain during labor and did not therefore require anesthesia (4). In the Dick-Read method the pregnant woman attends classes which provide a general orientation and regimen of exercises designed to prepare her for labor. The father also becomes actively involved. This preparation enables the mother, with the father's moral and physical support, to be an alert and active participant in the delivery room.

A similar method of natural childbirth was developed in the Soviet Union and introduced into Western countries by Fernand Lamaze (8). This method, known as the psychoprophylactic method (PPM), also involves classes and exercises. The mother is taught a series of breathing techniques upon which she concentrates during labor in order to diminish the sensation of pain.

Those who advocate natural childbirth believe that the preparatory procedures reduce anxiety and pain. It should be noted, however, that for the many women who find natural childbirth successful, there are a substantial number of others who require anesthesia, especially during difficult deliveries.

THE LEBOYER METHOD. Frederick Leboyer, a French physician, proposed procedural changes in delivery room management to make possible "birth without violence." The atmosphere should be quiet and soothing, the lighting soft. Harsh methods such as slapping the baby upon birth and the use of cold instruments should be abandoned. The umbilical cord is not to be cut until the baby can be placed on the mother's body where he can be gently massaged to stimulate breathing. After this the baby should be placed in a basin of warm water that simulates the fetal environment. All in all, Leboyer seeks to minimize the shock induced by the abrupt transition from the quiet warmth of the womb to the noisy, spacious outside world (9).

Prematurity. When a baby is born before completion of a full gestation period, the birth is considered to be premature. The precise definition of prematurity, however, is a subject upon which there is some disagreement. The majority view uses a combination of criteria, particularly birth weight and duration of the gestation period, to establish prematurity. A child born prior to the thirty-seventh week after fertilization, and who weighs less than 5½ pounds, is generally classified as premature.

The causes of prematurity are numerous; they include maternal infection, malnutrition, physical or emotional shock, and smoking. In many instances the cause of premature birth cannot be definitely established. Premature babies tend to develop more slowly than do full-term babies. There is also evidence that the earlier the baby is born, the more likely he is to have developmental defects. However, no definitive proof exists that premature babies show significant deviations from full-term babies by the time they reach adulthood.

In the past, premature babies were provided with excessive amounts of pure oxygen to combat anoxia. This led to a form of blindness known as retrolental fibroplasia. As the danger in this practice has become more widely known, the incidence of such cases of blindness has been greatly reduced.

Birth Injury. Physical and mental abnormalities may result from injury suffered by the baby during the process of birth.

Anoxia. For a variety of reasons, the supply of oxygen is sometimes drastically reduced or cut off entirely from the baby during delivery (anoxia), causing varying degrees of damage to the brain. In such instances the baby may die of suffocation, develop physical defects, or show mental retardation. Mild anoxia does not seem to have lasting effects.

Physical Injury. The baby may also suffer actual physical injury during birth. Brain damage may be the result of pressure on the head, particularly if the delivery is a difficult one, as in the case of a breech birth when the position of the fetus is reversed in the uterus.

Cerebral Palsy. Cerebral palsy, which is manifested by involuntary muscular movements and poor coordination, is caused by damage to the brain before or during birth. When the brain centers that govern motor abilities are damaged the child becomes seriously deficient in motor functioning. If the brain damage is extensive, the child may also suffer visual and intellectual impairment.

Minimal Brain Damage. The location, degree, and severity of brain damage suffered during birth determine whether the ensuing defects will be readily observable at birth or shortly after. In some instances, mild damage to brain cells is suspected despite the absence of positive neurological findings. Behavioral hyperactivity and some learning disorders that show up as the child develops are thought to be related to minimal brain dysfunction (MBD).

Blindness and Deafness. Bone fractures or hemorrhaging associated with a difficult delivery may cause damage to the sensory organs. The consequences of such injuries may be of short duration with no lasting or with minimal-lasting effects, or the injury may be severe enough to cause permanent damage to the eyes or ears. Blindness and deafness may also result from the mother's ingestion of a toxic or traumatic agent during the prenatal period. Any injury inflicted on the embryo, the fetus, or the baby during delivery that damages tissues, nerve centers, or other structures involved in seeing and hearing will impair functioning in these areas.

NEONATAL DEVELOPMENT

The neonatal period encompasses the beginning weeks of life. Some writers refer to the first month of life as the neonatal period, although others limit the period to the first week after birth.

Upon leaving the womb, the baby must immediately adapt to a

new environment and new bodily functioning in order to survive. There are only moments for the transition from receiving oxygen via the umbilical cord to breathing independently by inhaling and exhaling oxygen through the lungs. Similar shifts in functioning occur in connection with blood circulation, digestion, and temperature regulation as the neonate leaves the womb and becomes physiologically independent. In this section we will follow the transition from the fetal environment and trace the physical and emotional development of the newborn through the first month of life.

Physical Development. The average neonate weighs about 7 pounds (3+ kg) at birth and measures about 20 inches (51 cm). Some neonates present an unattractive appearance; not only may the face be wrinkled and the eyes puffy, but the head may appear elongated as a result of squeezing through the birth canal. Skin color is sometimes yellowish because of slight jaundice (which is normal), and bruises from the use of forceps may be noted. The neonate's head is large in relation to the trunk, and the feet, which are drawn up in a fetal position for the first few days, seem disproportionately long. The newborn has little fatty tissue other than the fat pads that line the cheeks; this absence of body fat adds to his frail appearance.

REFLEXES. As helpless as newborns seem to be, they possess a number of unlearned mechanisms that are protective and adaptive in nature. The *rooting* and *sucking reflexes* enable the neonate to take in nourishment, and the *withdrawal reflex* triggers defensive jerking of the feet away from stimuli. The neonate also exhibits a shielding motion of the hands when the head is touched. Other adaptive responses include *pupillary reflex,* permitting the eyes to respond to light and darkness; the *salivation reflex;* and the *vegetative reflexes,* which enable the neonate to swallow, sneeze, cough, regurgitate, hiccup, and yawn.

The newborn baby shows several motor reflexes which are significant in that positive responses indicate healthy subcortical functioning. Upon gentle stimulation of the sole of the neonate's foot, his toes will fan upward and outward. This is known as the *Babinski reflex*. Later in infancy this response reverses and the toes turn down in a curling position upon plantar stimulation. The *Moro reflex* demonstrates the baby's ability to respond to sudden movement or a loud noise. The baby first stretches out his arms and legs and then brings them together. Other reflexes of the neonate are the *grasping* and *swimming reflexes.* Later in infancy these latter two reflexes and the Moro reflex disappear as cortical functioning takes over. The Moro reflex is thought to reappear later as the startle reflex.

PHYSICAL NEEDS. Although the neonate comes into the world with a full complement of bodily structures (some not as fully mature as others) and is equipped to exist independently, he is nevertheless dependent upon outside assistance in order to survive. Just to possess sucking, swallowing, and rooting reflexes is not enough; the feeding process demands reinforcement of these reflexes by the mother. Some newborns require a high degree of stimulation during feeding periods; otherwise, they fail to suck vigorously. Others become frustrated by their inability to coordinate their nursing movements and require soothing. Since the neonate must take adequate nourishment during this early period in order to avoid weight loss, a patient and caring mother is extremely important to his welfare. Most neonates experience hunger approximately every three hours and require about eight feedings a day, with some variation according to individual preferences.

SLEEP HABITS. Most neonates sleep seventeen to twenty hours a day for about three hours at a time. Two kinds of neonatal sleep have been observed: regular sleep, a quiet relaxed rhythmic state, and irregular sleep, characterized by rapid eye movements (REM), uneven breathing, and restlessness. REM sleep is associated with dreaming in children and adults. It is difficult to imagine the dream content of newborn babies. Perhaps the existence of the physiological structure for dreaming at this early stage may be in preparation for use at a later date. It has also been proposed that REM activity may stimulate the development of the higher brain centers.

MOTOR CONTROL. The neonate is most inadequate with regard to motor control. Unlike the newborns of most mammals, the human newborn cannot lift himself shortly after birth but is dependent upon others to manipulate his body in order to achieve comfort. It is only toward the end of the first month of life that the infant begins to exert some motor control by lifting his chin when lying on his stomach. Some infants prefer to lie on their stomachs; others prefer to lie on their backs. They keep their fingers clenched in a fist position and cannot control hand movements other than to grasp reflexively at a pencil or finger when the palm is touched. Although some fetuses have been known to suck their fingers and continue to do so after birth, most neonates have difficulty in locating their mouths and need assistance to do so in the beginning.

RESPIRATION AND CIRCULATION. As the placenta begins to detach from the uterine wall, the source of oxygen is shut off, and the oxygen level in the neonate's blood decreases. At the same time, the carbon dioxide level increases. This triggers the breathing reflex, and immediately upon birth the baby takes a shallow breath. Some neonates need special stimulation to start breathing, and for this reason the baby is often given a slap on the bottom at birth. Crying forces air into the lungs, inflating them. A neonate's breathing is often irregular and diaphragmatic.

As soon as breathing begins, changes take place in the fetal circulation which force blood through the lungs. From this point on, the right ventricle of the heart pumps blood to the lungs, thus supplying them with oxygen. The neonate's heart beats rapidly, at a rate of 120 to 140 beats per minute.

DIGESTION. Although as a fetus the new individual received nourishment from his mother's blood, soon after birth he is able to shift to an entirely new feeding mode. The neonate sucks, swallows, digests, and eliminates wastes after birth without prior experience with these functions. Neonates show a slight weight loss during the first few days because of small nutritional intake and elimination of a greenish substance called *meconium,* as well as mucus and other wastes. Although the mother's milk does not begin to flow until a few days after birth, the breasts secrete a milky substance called *colostrum* which has some nutritive value. Sugar water is administered during the first few days of life to supplement breast milk or bottle formula. Many neonates develop mild jaundice which is evidenced by a yellowish skin color. This condition is due to improper functioning of the red blood cells or to the temporary deficiency of a liver enzyme called transferase. Neonate jaundice is usually of short duration. At about two or three weeks of age some babies develop colic (severe gastric pains), which lasts about three months. The causes of colic are not clear. Some authorities feel that it is due to tension or other psychological factors stemming from the mother-child relationship.

TEMPERATURE REGULATION. The neonate has little fatty tissue to provide insulation. Moreover, his sweat glands do not become operative until about thirty days after birth. Thus the neonate is extremely sensitive to cold or heat and requires protection until the temperature-regulating mechanisms begin to function.

IMMUNITY. Upon entrance into the germ-filled world, the neonate is protected by a supply of antibodies received from the mother during her last months of pregnancy. Although the baby is usually resistant to most infectious diseases for several months, respiratory infections and infections of the gastrointestinal tract are not uncommon during the first month of life.

SENSORY CAPACITIES. The neonate can see, hear, distinguish tastes, perceive sharp odors (ammonia, vinegar), and experience pain. Studies show that infants are able to discern faces from the moment of birth and that they can also respond to them (6). In a few days they can track a moving object with their eyes.

Newborns require and respond well to tactile (touch) stimulation and other forms of arousal. Rocking quiets the neonate, releasing motor tension.

SKELETAL DEVELOPMENT. The neonate's bones are soft and flexible at birth and not yet ossified. Near the top of the skull are soft spots called the *fontanels;* these disappear when the baby reaches one or two years of age, and bone tissue completely covers the brain. Bones harden at different rates; by the end of the neonatal stage, the neck bones and muscles have developed sufficiently to permit the baby to lift his chin, but it takes another four months for the baby to roll over.

HABITUATION. Can a neonate learn? Authorities feel that the process of habituation, of becoming used to a particular activity rather quickly, is a sign of neonatal learning. For example, when a baby first hears a particular sound he may react by blinking his eyes, by crying, or by manifesting a startlelike behavior. If the sound is repeated and becomes part of the background, the infant will be calmed by it rather than aroused. Some sounds, such as a mother's lullaby and the rhythmic action of a metronome, have a more calming effect on the baby than others. Some investigators suggest that any sound is better than no sound in soothing a neonate.

Emotional Response. Through the years psychologists have speculated about the neonate's capacity to respond emotionally. Some believe that physiological structures are too immature at this early period to permit any emotional responses beyond those of a reflexive nature. Others, such as Otto Rank, a psychoanalyst, place great emphasis on the birth trauma, theorizing that the severe anxiety suffered by the baby because of physical separation from his mother at birth becomes the basis for all future anxiety and neurotic behavior during childhood. The mother-child relationship is of great importance during the neonatal stage. A condition known as *marasmus* (Greek for "wasting away") has been observed in institutionalized babies (13). These babies become unresponsive and listless, even to the point of death, because of lack of maternal nurturance. It is felt by some that the physiological systems of the neonate deprived of personalized and loving attention fail to develop and the infant is actually unable to breathe, sleep, and suck properly. A mothering relationship, according to this viewpoint, stimulates the physiological processes during early life.

Although neonates may all seem to be alike at birth, individual characteristics begin to manifest themselves within a few hours and certainly within a few days. Nursery attendants are aware of differences in temperament in infants shortly after delivery. Some are more active than others; some cry more; some respond to stimuli more readily; some enjoy being picked up and held whereas others resist it. A number of studies have been made of personality differences appearing at birth. Alexander Thomas and his associates (14) hold that the environmental viewpoint expressed by theorists such as Margaret Ribble, René Spitz, and John Bowlby places a great burden on parents. Indeed, he argues, individual differences in children at an early age may influence parents as much as parents influence infants. According to Thomas, a child's behavior can be attributed in large part to innate characteristics, and parents should therefore not feel inadequate or guilty when a child does not respond to normally accepted methods of child rearing. It is preferable, he states, to acknowledge the difference in the temperament of the child and accommodate the child-rearing practices to his particular needs.

Neonates have a limited repertoire of emotional expression. When feeling distress from hunger or pain, they cry or become flushed or restless. Peter Wolff, who studied behavior in neonates, found that newborns show a smile reflex within two to twelve hours after delivery. Wolff could elicit smiles from babies during states of drowsiness by making various sounds. Social smiles, in response to seeing or hearing a person, occurred as early as the third week of life and could be distinguished from the earlier type of reflex smile (16).

4

Infancy: The First Eighteen Months

The course of human growth and development has been divided into periods for the purpose of study and discussion. Thus the time before birth is called the prenatal period; the first month after birth, the neonatal period. The subsequent childhood years are usually known as infancy, toddlerhood, the preschool years or early childhood, childhood or the middle years, and adolescence. Some authorities prefer different labels for these intervals. The years of middle childhood, for example, have also been called the latency years. Chronological groupings vary as well, so that the stage of toddlerhood, for instance, is sometimes incorporated into early childhood.

No matter how the years of development are categorized, however, these divisions are arbitrary, inasmuch as growth is a continuous process. Despite spurts and lags, children grow more or less steadily, and each child has his own timetable. The successive chronological periods overlap with regard to each child and vary from one child to another. Only broad trends and characteristics can be discerned, and while these trends form the basis for detailed analysis, they must be recognized to be only the generalizations that they are.

By the end of the second month of postnatal life the infant has a remarkable array of abilities and skills. Nevertheless, he is entirely dependent upon his caretakers. Visual ability is limited, and his responses, though selective, are more likely to be reflexive than self-determined. By the end of the first year and a half, however, a transformation will have taken place. During that time the infant will not only have grown in size and weight, but his bodily proportions will also have changed. The bones and muscles will have become stronger, and with continued neurological development the infant will gain increased control over his body. Motor development will progress from creeping, to standing with help, to unassisted walking. During the same time span the infant will have acquired some communicational skills. The cries of the neonatal period will become specific demand cries, and two-word phrases such as "go-bye" will be used. Mental development will be further demonstrated by an increased understanding of verbal and nonverbal communications, such as response to an order to "come" or to a facial expression that denotes reproof.

PHYSICAL DEVELOPMENT

Human growth and development is a gradual and complex process involving the close interrelationship of all body systems. By the time an infant is eighteen months of age he should have a well-defined, unique personality. That personality will represent the interaction of numerous forces, not the least of which is the physical growth of the organism from conception through the prenatal and neonatal periods and early infancy. The maturation of all bodily organs and of the muscular, skeletal, and central nervous systems has changed the nature and shape of the developing baby. These changes have also had a profound effect on the infant's relationship to his world. They have determined what he sees, hears, interprets, and learns, and how he uses that learning. They have also determined to a large degree how people react to him and how he responds to them. Thus the psychological self and the social self have evolved along with physical growth and maturation.

In the ensuing discussion of physical growth in infancy, developmental norms will be cited, but it must be kept in mind that such norms are simply statistical averages. There is no truly average child, that is, a child who meets the norm in all respects. An infant who cuts his first tooth at an earlier age than the expected average may lag behind his peers in motor development. It is nevertheless important to recognize the upper and lower limits of the normal range in the various aspects of growth, because an infant displaying marked and persistent deviations from these limits may require more careful observation. Such deviations may be indicative of problems that have a good chance of responding to remedial intervention.

Height. The infant grows rapidly in the early months of life; by the end of the first year he will be approximately 30 inches tall

(75+ cm), an increase of about one-half of his birth height. At two years of age he will measure approximately 34 inches (87 cm), almost half of his adult height.

As stated in Chapter 2, growth patterns change from age to age in accordance with the principle of *discontinuity of growth rate*. While the period of early infancy is characterized by rapid growth, the rate of growth decreases considerably after the baby passes his second birthday, and even more after the third birthday. Nevertheless, there are no interruptions in the steady upward gain in height until maturity is reached. While girls and boys tend to grow at almost the same rate, boys usually grow a little faster until about seven months of age, when girls take a slight lead until age four. There is no difference in growth rate from this age on until adolescence, when both sexes realize spurts in growth at different chronological ages. For all practical purposes the difference in the rate of growth between girls and boys is negligible. Girls, on the average, are slightly shorter than boys of the same age, except during adolescence when, for a short period, girls achieve an earlier growth spurt.

Body Proportions. The asynchronous growth patterns described in Chapter 2 can also be noted as the various parts of the body grow, and the child of eighteen months becomes not only taller but differently proportioned than the newborn. At birth, the baby seems to be more head than anything else; indeed, the head is about one-fourth of the total height of the baby. By the end of two years the infant's head is significantly smaller in proportion to the rest of the body, whereas the trunk and legs have markedly increased in length, and the chest has filled out. As a result of this pattern of cephalocaudal (head-to-foot) growth, the configuration of the body will change throughout childhood and adolescence until adult proportions are reached at maturity.

Weight. The infant grows heavier as he grows taller; by eighteen months of age he will have gained about eighteen pounds and weigh approximately 25½ pounds (11+ kg). At this age he weighs slightly less than one-fifth of what his weight will become at eighteen years of age.

Although all aspects of physical growth are susceptible to nonmaturational factors, weight is particularly sensitive to external conditions. Fad diets, nutritional standards, emotional factors, and eating habits all account for variations in weight, and for this reason, differences in weight norms are found in various parts of the world, particularly in areas of economic privation.

Skeletal Structure. The skeleton, the bony frame of the individual, develops from soft tissue during the prenatal and early postnatal periods of life. Through a process called ossification the softer cartilage is gradually replaced by bone. The skeletal frame of the infant contains many spaces that will fill in as bones grow and move into place. The six soft spots, or fontanelles, in the skull remain for many months. Because the bones of the young baby are so soft and pliable, they are susceptible to malformation and deformity.

Different bones grow at different rates; they move into their proper places and fuse at different times in the life cycle. The growth and development of the skeleton follows the same sequential patterns in all individuals. Consequently, skeletal age is a more accurate indication of development than many other measurements. Standard measures of skeletal development are available for bones of the wrist, pelvis, knees, and ankles.

Teeth. The infant's first teeth (deciduous teeth), which were already forming in the gums during the prenatal period, make their appearance at about six months of age. The lower central incisors erupt first. By the end of the first year the baby has approximately eight "milk teeth." These primary teeth continue to appear for the first three years. Girls, who generally have a faster maturational timetable, are slightly ahead of boys in the development of permanent teeth, which begin to replace the "baby" teeth at about six years of age. This process continues during childhood and adolescence. The third molars or wisdom teeth may erupt anywhere from seventeen to thirty years of age.

Central Nervous System. From birth until about two years of age, the baby undergoes extensive neurological development. During this critical period of growth, the infant is susceptible to damage to the brain and nerves as a result of illness, traumatic injury, toxicity, or malnutrition.

Unlike other organ systems, the central nervous system, comprised of the brain and the spinal cord, is developmentally incomplete at birth. The brain, which in the newborn is only one-sixth of its final weight, undergoes extensive growth during the first two years of life. By the time the baby is one year old the brain has doubled in size. As the brain begins to grow, the infant gains more control over his body. Myelinization (sheathing) of the neural fibers makes nerve impulses less diffuse. Sensory functioning (seeing and hearing) is well established by six months of age. Marked development of the motor areas of the brain cortex that control the head, hands, upper trunk, and legs has taken place by six months of age. As these cortical areas mature during the second year of life, the baby becomes more physically and neurologically proficient in motor activities.

Motor Development. Bone calcification, increase in muscle tissue, development of the cerebral cortex, and myelinization of neural fibers are all prerequisites for motor development. With the appearance of these biological foundations, the infant begins to demonstrate an increasing degree of voluntary and coordinated motor activity.

There are many published norms and developmental scales for motor skills (11). Although these scales are far from uniform, they all agree on the sequence in which the various milestones are reached. The baby first turns from his stomach to his back at about five months of age, and is able to reverse the process within a month or so. Creeping activities start in the seventh or eighth month, and toward the end of the first year the baby is usually able to stand alone. Unassisted walking begins between twelve and fifteen months of age, and by the end of the second year the baby walks fairly well and can climb stairs.

Motor skill increases with practice. The baby's ability to reach for and then securely hold an object, to purposely release an object from his grasp, and to pick up small objects with his fingers develops slowly throughout the first year.

As the period of infancy comes to a close the child is a relatively facile and mobile individual. He is well on the way to achieving the variety of motor skills which, in time, will be smooth and automatic.

MENTAL DEVELOPMENT

Inevitably, a number of aspects of physical growth intertwine with mental development, since the infant is a total organism, not merely a mind, a body, or a personality. Therefore we must be aware of the interrelationship that exists between the growing and unfolding physical and neurological components of the child, and the child's sensory, perceptual, learning, problem-solving qualities.

Mental development encompasses the emergence and growth of physical structures such as the brain, the sensory apparatus, and the communicational faculties. It also includes the process through which the child uses these structures to become aware of and understand the world around him.

The senses pick up stimuli and transmit impulses to the brain through the nervous system. The brain deciphers, collates, and interprets the meaning of the stimuli, and then sends back a response. For example, spoken words are heard, understood, and responded to. This act involves perception, memory, cognition, comprehension, physical coordination, and a variety of other linguistic and interpersonal skills. Mental development is the process by which these skills are achieved.

Perception. The infant makes contact with his world through his sensory apparatus. Even in the earliest days and weeks of infancy, stimuli are being received by the visual, auditory, olfactory, and tactile senses. At birth the infant's sensations are somewhat diffuse, but very quickly these sensations become more specific and take on meaning. Through the process called perception, the infant organizes and interprets the evidence of his senses and formulates a working model of the world.

VISUAL PERCEPTION. There are marked biological differences between the eye of the newborn and that of the adult. The infant eye will eventually double in size and weight. Within a few hours after birth infants are able to follow visual stimuli at close range, but it will be three or four months before they are able to shift their degree of focus and accommodate to objects at varying distances. The newborn's visual acuity is good but limited and will improve throughout infancy and childhood until maximum acuity of 20/20 to 20/15 on the Snellen scale is reached at age ten.

Very young babies have been found to look for light in darkness and to discern form—for example, a spot or a triangle in a formless field. Neonates have demonstrated the ability to perceive distances by their avoidance responses to approaching (looming) objects. Six-week-old infants can make spatial discriminations and tend to prefer patterned to plain surfaces and three-dimensional to two-dimensional objects. Although these skills appear in the earliest weeks of life, they improve markedly after the second month.

DEPTH PERCEPTION. Along with the development of the ability to focus comes the development of depth perception. This has been demonstrated by the Walk-Gibson *visual cliff* experiments which utilize a thick sheet of plate glass to create the illusion of a cliff (16). Babies who were set upon a platform on the glass refused to crawl to their mothers if the path they had to take crossed over the "cliff." They responded readily to their mothers' calls, however, when the glass did not present an illusion of depth. In these experiments infants younger than six months were less likely to avoid crawling over the visual cliff, indicating, in all probability, that they do not have the ability to perceive depth and consequently do not react to this perceptual illusion.

PATTERN PERCEPTION. Infants respond early to the human face, although at first they may react merely to a head and eyes or even to a scrambled version of the face. The ability to discriminate and the degree of response develop rapidly, so that by about four months no stimulus less than a correct combination of facial elements will elicit a response. In time the infant becomes even more selective; at five or six months he will react differently to a smiling face than to an angry one, and later still, he will recognize familiar faces.

OBJECT PERMANENCE. It is evident that the infant has a remarkable array of visual perceptual abilities. These abilities continue to improve as the physical structures involved in vision mature. With neurological growth and increased experience, connections and associations are made between different visual events. Thus, at eight months the child begins to be aware that there is a permanence to objects, that they do not just vanish when they are out of sight. The concept of object permanence is described by Piaget (13). The delight a child of this age takes in playing peekaboo-type games, in which an object (whether it be a toy or mother) appears, disappears, and then reappears, illustrates the interrelationship between physical, mental, and social development.

AUDITORY PERCEPTION. Newborn babies are sensitive to sounds of different frequency, intensity, and duration. Experiments show that almost from birth infants can differentiate between a bell and a buzzer, and can determine whether a particular sound comes from the right or left side. From the earliest weeks of life they can tell the difference between the sounds of certain consonants. It is thus likely that they can appreciate many of the shadings of feeling and meaning conveyed by speech. Babies seem to prefer the sounds of the human voice to other sounds, especially low and rhythmic tones and words. With the clear establishment of the ability to locate sound at six months of age, the baby begins to respond to meaningful and familiar words. In so doing, the infant is revealing the personal interpretation he is attaching to vocal sounds. He is now associating specific sounds with such significant components of his life as mother, food, love, and anger.

OTHER SENSES. From birth, babies can distinguish between and react to odors and tastes. They quickly turn their heads away from sharp odors such as ammonia and alcohol and turn toward pleasant ones. Their taste preference is for sweet substances, followed in order by sour and then salty substances. Bitterness evokes active avoidance responses. By six months of age infants develop clear-cut food preferences.

The sense of touch is also present very early in life. Upon tactile stimulation, babies respond with the Babinski and other reflexes. They withdraw from pain stimuli such as a pinprick but are less sensitive to pain at birth than they are a week later. There is some evidence that girls are more sensitive to pain and tactile stimulation than boys.

The general sense of touch and the baby's varying responses to it increase rapidly in the early days of infancy and become integrated into mental and social development processes.

Cognition. Mental activity, which includes the processing of perceptual stimuli, memory storage, interpreting of sensory input, reasoning, and the manipulation of ideas, is characterized as cognition. The process by which individuals use schemata, symbols, and concepts in order to know and understand their world, to learn, to think, and to solve problems is encompassed within the meaning of cognition.

Rudimentary cognitive skills are present at birth and may even start to develop in prenatal life, since the fetus as well as the neonate and infant is surrounded by stimuli. The ability to select which stimuli will be permitted to intrude and receive a measure of attention and which will be screened out develops gradually.

SCHEMATA. As the baby matures he develops mental skills which can be described as functional units. These skills, in turn, facilitate the development of cognition. One of the earliest of these units is the schema. The schema may be thought of as a constantly changing mental representation, blueprint, map, or memory pattern, used by the infant to organize and familiarize himself with his surroundings. In early infancy schemata are vague, such as that of the human face, but as the baby is exposed to new stimuli and new experiences he develops more specific, definitive, and valid representations of the elements of his world.

Although schemata facilitate the baby's orientation to and familiarity with his environment, they are merely shorthand representations, just as a road on a map represents but does not look like an actual highway. As the infant matures he begins to construct more specific and detailed memories of a room, a person, or an event. Soon he can evoke *images,* which are clearer and more recognizable representations than are schemata. Both schemata and images, particularly the former, in very early life provide the basis for learning and for reacting to new experiences.

HABITUATION. When, through repeated exposure, a child becomes accustomed to and familiar with certain stimuli (a light, a sound, a pattern) he tends to lose interest; he is said to have become habituated. This phenomenon is possible because of the mental faculties already operative in the infant after a few weeks of life. He has, as we have seen, the ability to perceive; he can pay attention; and he has the ability to remember, for memory is required in order to become accustomed to or bored with a particular stimulus.

Dishabituation occurs when the baby's attention is rearoused by introduction of a new stimulus following the onset of habituation. The greatest likelihood of interest rearousal takes place when the new stimulus is moderately different from the habituated stimulus. The baby's attentiveness increases with stimuli that are somewhat familiar yet different, once again implying a degree of recall ability.

As the infant grows older his ability to habituate becomes greater. It is this ability which enables individuals to disregard so many of the sounds and sights in their environment—for example, the noise of airplanes and automobiles, and the dozens of faces encountered each day on the street.

Piaget's Sensorimotor Stage. Piaget, as indicated earlier, finds cognitive ability evolving out of a continual process of adaptation. The individual takes in new objects and events that he encounters in his experience. These he *assimilates,* or incorporates into his existing schemata and ideas. In seeking a balance or *equilibration* between discrepant or novel stimuli and that which he has already assimilated, the person *accommodates* by modifying existing schemata and ideas to include the new experience. In this way the person takes in, adapts, and learns. In Piagetian theory, development consists of a shift from lower to progressively higher levels of equilibration as maturation and experience increase.

From the first day of life, the baby's cognitive development is continuous. Infancy, from birth to eighteen months, corresponds roughly to the first of Piaget's four stages of cognitive growth, the sensorimotor stage. This period, in turn, is divided into six developmental stages (10).

Stage 1 (birth to one month): *reflexes and egocentrism.* The infant is preoccupied with his own sensations and does not distinguish self from others. His actions stem from inborn reflexes (rooting, sucking, and grasping) and random movements.

Stage 2 (one to four months): *primary circular actions.* The baby repeats satisfying bodily activities that arise out of reflexive movements, random actions, and external stimuli. Although these acts are repeated for their own sake, the infant is beginning to define the limits of his own body.

Stage 3 (four to eight months): *secondary circular reactions.* The baby now repeats actions that create interesting effects, thereby indicating the ability to anticipate. Behavior is less and less accidental. Although a sound (of a rattle or a bell) may have been produced by chance movements, the baby repeats the movement that caused the sound. Thus he is beginning to make a distinction between himself and his surroundings.

Stage 4 (eight to twelve months): *coordination of secondary reactions.* Intentional activity has become an increasingly large part of the infant's behavior. He now uses learned responses to obtain desired results, and he is aware of the permanence of objects.

Stage 5 (twelve to eighteen months): *tertiary circular reactions.* The baby now uses trial and error and makes active attempts at solving problems new ways. This behavior Piaget termed "directed groping."

Stage 6 (eighteen to twenty-four months): *internal experimentation.* Problem-solving behavior is now internalized, that is, the child resorts to mental considerations of a problem before he acts. This is the beginning of symbolic representation.

Piagetian theory sees the infant moving gradually and sequentially from an exclusive focus on self to an awareness of his environment. Reflexive, random behavior gives way to self-directed, purposeful action. The baby shifts from a physical-motor orientation to a mental understanding of his world.

Learning. The foregoing discussion makes it clear that the infant possesses the tools for learning early in life. He can perceive and remember. The ability to use symbols and concepts is still well beyond him, but the steps toward accomplishing those skills are being taken. Very young babies have been taught, through the use of conditioning techniques, to seek out a bottle from the right or left side depending on the sound stimulus (bell or buzzer). They are able to learn and respond to the presence or the absence of an object. At about eight or nine months of age, as was noted previously, they learn that objects have the quality of permanence, although long before this age, at sixteen to eighteen weeks, babies can be taught to follow the path of an object that disappears and then reappears in a regular trajectory. Such relatively simple learning capacity has been amply demonstrated in young infants.

Although much of this learning appears to depend on conditioning, in which behavior is reinforced by environmental change, there is evidence that infant learning may also be self-generated for the sake of some inner-determined reward such as the pleasure derived from solving a problem. Learning, in infants as well as in adults, is a complicated process, and it does not always follow the laws of conditioning. Piaget and others have said that the child's mind is not simply a receptor and responder to stimuli from the environment, that the mind very early in life develops the ability to organize stimulus input according to rules. Thus the baby interprets the meaning of a stimulus within the context of the existing rules and patterns, and then responds accordingly.

Learning starts from the first moments of a baby's life. The capacity to learn and learning itself are inextricably tied to maturation and experience, the former playing a less dominant role as the individual approaches maturity. Learning, however, does not occur in the abstract. It occurs in relation to specific people, events, objects, or ideas. Early in life the baby learns that the object in front of him is a part of himself: his hand. He distinguishes his mother's face from other faces and learns the meanings of the different expressions she exhibits. By the end of infancy he has learned to walk. He has found some things that please him and has learned how to obtain pleasure. He has also become aware of some things that frighten him. He has learned elementary communicational techniques, primarily nonverbal. He has yet to develop the understanding of symbols and, except in the most primitive ways, he cannot conceptualize. The foundations for development of concepts, however, are present.

Language. Achievement of language skills is one of the milestones in the development of the human being. Language acquisition is intertwined with cognitive, social, and personality development. The baby utters sounds from the first day of life. These are generally physiologically based cries that accompany acts of eating, breathing, and similar functions. In the first few weeks new sounds make their appearance. Gradually, sounds become associated with experiences and events and are differentiated with relation to pain, hunger, and pleasure.

Infant vocalization known as babbling starts at about five or six months of age. The baby at this time repetitively utters meaningless sounds of more than one syllable combining vowels and consonants (for example, mamamama or bibibi). At about nine months the baby begins to produce sounds that are organized or patterned, and by the time he is one year old, he has made a sound that is recognizable as a word. His first words generally designate objects or people, but gradually the words expand in meaning to include requests, demands, and relatively complex communications. The spoken word "pop" may mean "I want a lollipop" or "Where is my lollipop?" or "Big noise pop" or any other number of things unrelated to the word itself. By eighteen or twenty-four months combinations of words make their appearance, usually in the form of such two-word sentences as "Me good" or "Go-bye."

Two further points should be made with regard to language development. First, the sounds and vocalizations made by the baby from his first days of life—crying, cooing, gurgling, and babbling—are not the product of learning. This is evident from the fact that even deaf babies make those sounds. Second, at any given time in early development the infant understands many more words than he can produce. He knows what "sleep," "eat," or "go for walk" means long before he can articulate those sounds in a meaningful or purposive way.

PERSONALITY DEVELOPMENT

Personality may be defined as the stable attributes of the individual which make him unique and different from all other individuals. It is the product of many aspects of human functioning—physical, mental, emotional, and social—how they interrelate, and how they interact with the environment. This section will trace personality development during the first eighteen months of life.

Early Determinants. There have been many attempts to rate the significance of the factors and forces that determine personality. However, it is difficult, if not impossible, to single out any one force as dominant. Each potentially influential event or circumstance varies in the effect it has on a particular infant's personality development, depending on the other influences in his life. For example, poor motor coordination may cause extreme feelings of masculine inadequacy in a boy born into a family and community where athletic prowess is highly valued in boys. It may, on the other hand, have little significance if the boy lives with a family in a community where physical skill has a low priority and where language and intellectual ability are prized. The loss of a parent may be extremely traumatic if no substitute parent is available; it may be of lesser consequence if there is a close family constellation with a warm, loving grandparent to replace the parent.

Among the influential factors in the shaping of personality are those associated with the culture or society and the time in history into which a baby is born, his physical constitution, the situational-accidental happenings he encounters, and the interpersonal relationships in his life.

CONSTITUTIONAL DETERMINANTS. One of the major influences in the development of personality is the individual's physical makeup. This includes not only the main biological systems but also the broad spectrum of physical assets and limitations such as physical appearance, disability, and motor coordination.

From the moment of birth, babies are constitutionally different; they differ in height, weight, appearance, activity level, and degree of physical response to the environment. Some babies are very active; others are quiet. Some are easily excited and aroused, whereas others are more placid and respond slowly to stimulation. Babies differ in heartbeat responses to tension and in the way they react under physiological stress. There is much variation in how readily they can be quieted or soothed. From birth they seem to prefer certain quieting and soothing ministrations over others.

Regardless of whether or not constitutional differences in babies are caused by genetic, prenatal, or postnatal factors, the foundations for personality development are present at the beginning of life. It is not simply that these constitutional differences lead to physically different children who therefore reveal differences of personality based on those constitutional variations. Inasmuch as personality evolves out of many interrelated forces, constitutional characteristics such as degree of excitability or soothability evoke differential reactions in parents. These reactions in turn affect how the baby feels and responds and, in time, will be part of his developing self-image, with all its implications for personality development.

Differences between infants in rate of growth, attainment of motor skills, skeletal structure, and subsequent ability to communicate become apparent as babies mature. Facial features take on definition, and the baby may come to resemble some member of the family. In this total growth process constitutional characteristics are receiving approval or disapproval, overt or covert, from parents and others. The baby's looks and abilities create pleasure, satisfaction, or anxiety in parents whose related responses are communicated to the baby and others. Thus not only the constitutional factors themselves but parental response to them become significant forces in the formation of personality in the young child.

CULTURAL DETERMINANTS. Babies do not, of course, grow and develop in isolation. They live in families which in turn live in a particular community, region, or country and belong to a particular social class or culture. The culture, with all its divisions, determines to a major extent the traits the family will value in its children. The culture inculcates in its members attitudes toward aggression, cleanliness, competition, sex, and a multitude of other feelings and behavioral characteristics that are part of everyday living. The "culturization" of the individual starts at birth. In some societies babies are slung across the mother's body and carried about constantly;

there is a close physical communion between mother and child. In others, babies are carried only when they need to be fed or moved, emphasizing the physical separation between the two. Older children sometimes are the custodians of infants. In some cultures babies are spoken to and played with; in others they are left largely to their own devices. Infants are encouraged to become self-sufficient, assertive, and aggressive in some cultures, while in others, qualities of dependency, gentleness, and passivity are fostered. Thus do such personality components as attitudes toward people and the world at large evolve out of the framework of society's management of the baby.

Gradually infants are fitted into the mold of their society; their personality traits are expected to conform to those of their elders. This is not to say that all personalities in each culture are alike. There are different ways of being self-sufficient, industrious, or aggressive. Similarly, different social groups vary in the degree to which conformity is enforced and deviation is tolerated. In any event, individual personality characteristics vary, to some extent, from individual to individual whether they fit or deviate from applicable social norms.

SITUATIONAL OR ACCIDENTAL DETERMINANTS. Another category of determinants influencing personality development includes the numerous events and situations encountered by the individual during the course of his daily life. They may include such circumstances as proximity to the sea or the mountains, and conditions of economic hardship or advantage. Other events of an accidental nature may happen only once but may have extremely traumatic effects. Examples of such events are the witnessing of a violent act, involvement in a serious automobile collision, or experiencing a natural disaster such as a flood or earthquake. Situations of this type may have significant impact on the growing infant and child, resulting in internalized reactions and traits which then become influential in the formation of personality characteristics.

INTERPERSONAL DETERMINANTS. The influence often considered most crucial in the development of personality is the significant people in the child's life. In American society, the baby's parents and siblings are closest to him. This situation prevails in many other societies and cultures, although frequently the family is larger than the American family and includes an assortment of relatives. In many parts of the world, including America and Europe, the baby is sometimes cared for by an older sibling.

Whether they are natural or surrogate parents, those entrusted with the child's immediate care play a critical role in personality development. The following concepts represent some significant theoretical positions suggested in this regard.

Basic Trust. Erik Erikson sees the first year of life as the time when the individual develops a basic trust or mistrust of his environment (7). Whether a baby feels secure or insecure, confident or helpless, depends on the extent to which his needs are met by those responsible for his care. It is these feelings, vague at first, that determine how he sees the world: as potentially pleasant and fulfilling or as frustrating and threatening.

Attachment and Dependence. According to some theoreticians, the manner in which the caretaker (usually the mother) nurtures the baby during the peak dependency period has a major impact on the child's personality development. Erikson, as stated above, traced the development of trust to the role of parents in satisfying the baby's physical and psychological needs. Freud designated infancy as the oral stage in which the mouth is the focus of need satisfaction and tension release. It is part of the mother's role to provide sufficient oral gratification for normal personality development. Personality characteristics formed during this period of dependency may persist throughout life, according to Freudian theory.

Insights into human dependency needs have been found in animal behavior. Konrad Lorenz, the ethologist, studied the attachment of goslings to their mothers (12). He found that during a critical period of development, a gosling will become *imprinted* on the first moving object it sees, which under normal circumstances is the mother duck. Similarly, infants tend to form attachments to early caretakers.

John Bowlby believes that the attachment process has been a crucial factor throughout evolution (3). He states that both baby and mother have within them the mechanisms that lead to reciprocal behavior. The baby's smile and cooing please the mother, and she responds with smiles and baby talk. The baby's cries evoke concern, and the mother tries to meet the baby's needs. Thus an attachment develops. Bowlby further argues that babies who do not demonstrate the kind of behavior that elicits caretaker concern and response are likely to suffer deprivation and form poor attachment bonds. In fact, he theorizes, in early human evolution, such infants perished while those with loud cries or other attention-getting behavior survived. However, it should be pointed out that while each baby and mother may have varying degrees of attention-getting and responding behaviors, some babies who cry and smile infrequently may nevertheless receive adequate mothering. In such instances the mother's level of response may be high, thus compensating for the lack of demanding behavior in the baby.

Contact Comfort. Although dependency may well lead to attachment, Harry Harlow concluded from his experiments that the infant does not necessarily become attached to the person who satisfies his hunger, as had been suggested by some authorities (8). Harlow studied attachment behavior by providing newborn monkeys with two surrogate mother models. One motherlike figure was a bare wire frame; the other a wire frame covered with a soft terry-cloth material. A bottle with a nipple was attached to both models. The monkeys were divided into two groups, one of which received feedings from the wire "mother" and the other from the terry-cloth "mother." Feeding and nonfeeding surrogates were available to all of the monkeys. Harlow found that the monkeys spent most of their time clinging to the terry-cloth "mother" regardless of which "mother" provided its food. He therefore concluded that attachment was not a conditioned response to feeding, but rather it was associated with the baby monkey's need for physical closeness and softness. Babies ordinarily obtain this kind of comfort by clinging to a natural mother; in the experiments, the terry-cloth surrogate provided more comfort closeness than did the wire figure and was chosen for protection and support.

Harlow's studies not only called into question the previously accepted concepts about dependency and attachment but also demonstrated that baby monkeys need a total mothering experience in order to develop normally. When the monkeys under study attained maturity, they were markedly different from monkeys reared with their natural mothers in community with other monkeys. Some exhibited autistic behavior, sexual problems, and difficulties in relating to their own offspring. He concluded that a growing monkey required more than food and tactile comfort to develop into a normal adult.

Emotions. Since emotions are such an important factor in personality development, we will discuss here the nature of emotional response and consider the various kinds of emotional expression that appear in infancy.

NATURE OF EMOTIONS. While it is difficult to formulate a definition of emotional behavior acceptable to all psychologists, the layman has no difficulty in recognizing emotional experiences. Fear, anxiety, joy, and love are emotions that most people have known. All emotional responses have a number of common characteristics. First of all, they are the product of the endocrine glands, the nervous system, and the sense organs. Stimuli evoking an emotional response can originate outside the person (a loud noise, the smell of food, or spoken words) or within the person (the memory of events). Emotions are involuntary, and this characteristic distinguishes them from cognitive reactions. Although they may be psychologically denied and the behavior they evoke may be controlled, emotions cannot be voluntarily summoned or dismissed. Emotions range in degree, intensity, and quality; slight irritation and intense rage may differ only in degree of expression. Finally, the stimuli that elicit emotions appear to be socioculturally determined. Babies become conditioned to a variety of stimuli as they grow into adulthood. Food likes and dislikes, fear of mice, and reactions to such words and phrases as "communism," "America," or "I love you" are but a few examples of stimuli that produce conditioned emotional responses.

EMOTIONAL STATES IN INFANCY. Emotions under study in adults may be described by the individuals experiencing them or may be inferred by the psychologist from the individual's behavior. A person may say he feels angry, or his loud voice, red face, and shaking fist demonstrate his anger. In determining emotional states in young infants, judgment must be made on the basis of such behavioral clues as movements, vocalizations, and heart and respiration rates. The newborn exhibits many bodily movements under varying conditions. Although these involuntary movements are frequently thought to indicate excitement, they are more likely to be related to the maturing of physiological structures. Nevertheless there is evidence that babies are capable of emotional expression very early in life. Caution must be exercised, however, in relating particular behavioral activity to emotional origins. The baby's "smile" may actually denote a digestive reaction rather than an expression of emotion.

Early psychological thinking assumed that babies are born with the capacity for three basic emotions: fear, rage, and love. Subsequent study of the newborn has not corroborated this position. The presence of some emotions, though, has been inferred from the manner in which newborn babies react to different stimuli. Very young babies habituate; that is, they lose interest in repeated stimuli. This suggests that infants experience boredom. Their heartbeat and respiration rates increase in the presence of such seemingly threatening stimuli as a looming object; thus they seem to be experiencing fear. Babies can be soothed by picking them up, moving, or swaddling them. All these responses suggest the presence of rudimentary emotional states during infancy.

K. M. Bridges developed a timetable of approximate ages at which emotions are differentiated (4). The earliest responses exhibited by infants, according to Bridges, are reactions to pleasant and unpleasant stimuli, but it requires about three months of growth before the baby evidences the emotions termed distress, excitement, and delight. Fear, disgust, and anger can be discerned by six months, and such positive feelings as elation and affection are manifested by the time a baby is a year old. By eighteen months, the entire range of emotional response is present, including jealousy and affection.

The gradual development of emotional responses as charted by Bridges is not universally accepted. According to Freud, Erikson, Bowlby, and others, emotional mechanisms are functioning very early in life. They see basic trust, oral satisfaction, and attachment displayed during the earliest months of infancy. The emotional bases for these phenomena may be assumed then to predate Bridges' timetable. Anxiety, for example, an emotional state that underlies many theories on the origins of psychological disorders, can be detected within the first few months of infancy.

As infancy comes to a close, the baby is at a beginning stage of emotional development. In time he will differentiate more feelings and express them in many ways. The impulsive expression of emotions during infancy will eventually give way to emotional control. As the infant grows, and he experiences and learns, the content of his emotional life will expand and become enriched.

Effects of Early Life Experiences. Many studies have attempted to demonstrate the relationship between early life experiences and psychological development (15). Some investigators have explored the effects of trauma and deprivation; others have examined the effects of early experiences on mental, linguistic, and cognitive development.

EARLY DEPRIVATION. It would not be humane to deliberately expose infants to conditions of neglect in order to examine the long-term effects of early maternal deprivation. However, some investigators have been able to undertake such research by observing institutionalized babies who unfortunately became separated from their parents early in life. Studies of such infants show that they developed severe mental, motor, and psychological deficits, despite receiving adequate physical care. The infants also exhibited signs of withdrawal and depression. According to such research, early maternal deprivation can lead to serious and irreversible mental, physical, and emotional damage to the child (14).

Other studies have shown that when deprived babies are placed in nurturing environments, mental and emotional impairment can sometimes be reversed. Most authorities agree that early deprivation produces personality damage which can be irreversible if remedial intervention is not provided relatively early in life.

EARLY STIMULATION. In the past few years increased attention has been given to the effects of early environmental stimulation on the mental and personality development of the child. D. O. Hebb postulates the formation of neural structures he calls "cell assemblies," the simplicity or complexity of which depends on the amount of environmental stimulation the baby receives (9). These neural structures, he believes, are the bases for later higher-level cognitive functions. Thus, babies who are continually exposed to stimulating verbalization, social relationships, and play objects will develop the potential for higher-level functioning. Conversely, babies growing up in relatively barren environments will have less complex cell assemblies and will consequently be less capable of intricate mental functioning. A similar position is taken by Benjamin Bloom, who believes that lack of early stimulation results in irreversible intellectual limitations in later life (2).

Burton White and his associates agree that the foundations for mental, linguistic, and personal competence are laid down in the earliest months (17). They found that the more the infant is exposed to social experiences the greater the level of competency in later life. Among the most crucial of experiences are those which encourage the child to participate in live conversations (not on television or radio) directed toward him, to freely explore his home surroundings, and to interact with responsive adults.

SOCIAL DEVELOPMENT

One of the major consequences of the baby's physical, mental, and personality development is his entrance into the world of people. This section will trace the child's progress from the dependency of early infancy to the middle of the second year, by which time the baby has begun to play an active, reciprocal role with family members and other people around him.

Early Foundations. From birth, the baby interacts socially with his parents as they clothe and feed him. In the earliest weeks of life, the baby does not show any clear-cut reactions to these encounters. In a very short time, however, he begins to respond to social overtures; instead of staring blankly, he focuses on his mother's face. At first he is not responding to his mother as an individual, but rather to the schema of a human face. Gradually, however, he begins to discriminate facial characteristics, so that by twenty weeks, he recognizes specific features (the eyes, the mouth, the nose) as part of a face with which he interacts.

There is some evidence that babies as young as six months may distinguish between male and female faces, and between familiar and unfamiliar faces. At this point also, they begin to show anxiety in the presence of strangers. By nine or ten months of age, *stranger anxiety* is well established. Concurrently, advanced perceptual growth enables the infant to move into the social environment surrounding him. He plays pat-a-cake and he tries to imitate the ordinary sounds and behaviors that he hears and sees.

Smiling. The smile of the four-month-old baby who actively responds to external objects, faces, and sounds is quite different from the reflexive smile of the neonate. At this age, the baby responds to all manner of stimuli, particularly if movement is involved and if the moving object is a face or resembles a face. At about seven months the baby becomes selectively responsive, showing greater preference for primary caregivers. He smiles at parents and other close relatives, but exhibits wariness when strangers approach.

In time, the baby's smile becomes a significant part of his social repertoire. It enables him to obtain attention and affection, and provides him with a powerful means of social communication.

Vocalization. The baby's early vocalizations become integral elements in the socializing process. The child's cooing and gurgling, and sounds of annoyance and rage, all have an impact on his relationship to parents and others in his environment. In a subsequent chapter we will discuss early vocalization as a foundation for the development of language.

Early Socializing Influences. The growing infant is exposed to countless social stimuli that are part of the essential acts of caretaking. Such activities as bathing, toileting, feeding, and playing form an early prototype or model of the social world and the social relationships of later life. The feelings the baby develops toward his parents and siblings as they play with him and care for him become generalized to others. During these early months, the baby develops a foundation for the growth of social attitudes. The security gained through the parent-child interaction in infancy provides the child with the emotional strength he needs to cope with more complex social situations later in life. Thus, the infant develops social adaptability.

Peer Relationships. Throughout infancy the baby's social world is peopled primarily with adults and older children. They minister to him and play with him, but he does not meet them on equal terms.

Infants below one year of age usually respond to infants of like age as they do to objects. They seem to prefer to interact with adults. After one year of age they react to peers superficially. Conflicts may arise over playthings. Between fourteen and eighteen months of age, peer interest increases; the earliest signs of cooperative peer interaction, however, do not appear until the latter part of the second year.

Child Care. The infant's social development is integrally related to the culture in which he grows up and to the family which imparts the norms and values of that culture. Child-care techniques used by parents are reflections of both their social backgrounds and their particular personalities.

CULTURAL AND CLASS DIFFERENCES. During the early months of life, and for some time to come, the baby's immediate surroundings comprise his world. That small world conveys to him whether babies are desired and valued, or are merely accepted and tolerated. The infant quickly learns whether he can rely on his caretakers to meet his needs in a regular and consistent manner, or whether he must cry incessantly to gain attention. In other words, he learns early in life whether he can relax and trust those around him, or whether he must develop more demanding and aggressive social qualities.

Infant-care approaches reflect the differences in each society's life styles and expectations. A child grows to adulthood surrounded by constant reminders of that life style and those expectations. For example, Caudill and Plath reported that it is rare for Japanese infants to sleep alone; if they do not share a bed with their parents, they sleep with siblings (6). This practice may well continue into adulthood. Such sleeping arrangements may then be considered among the factors leading to a high degree of interdependence within the Japanese family setting and beyond. These customs are in marked contrast to those of American parents, who rear their children to be self-sufficient. Even more independent and mobile at an early age are the children of the Eskimos of northeastern Canada, whose life revolves around hunting (1).

As techniques vary from culture to culture, so they vary from one social class to another. Babies born into poor families experience infancy and parenting differently than children from middle-class or affluent homes. Children of the poor are affected by the tangible and intangible consequences of poverty. Not only do they eat less, but they are also exposed to parental attitudes rooted in the poverty milieu. The sense of helplessness in the face of powerful economic forces, the limited options open to them, and the imminence of disaster are all major factors in the world of a baby growing up among the poor.

INFANT FEEDING PRACTICES. Throughout most parts of the world, breast-feeding remains the standard mode of infant feeding. In the industrialized Western countries, however, bottle feeding has largely replaced, or serves as a supplement to, breast-feeding. While the controversy over the comparative advantages of one method over the other continues, there is increasing indication that breast milk provides immunological protection for the baby (5). There is, however, no clear-cut evidence that one practice is superior to the other as far as psychological development is concerned. The mother's own feelings about breast-feeding and intimacy with the infant may well be extensions of her other attitudes toward mothering, babies, and interpersonal relationships. These considerations may be more crucial in determining the child's eventual psychological development than choice of nursing or bottle feeding during infancy. However, with the renewed interest in natural motherhood, more women are turning to breast-feeding today.

In most parts of the world, the infant's signal of hunger and the mother's readiness to satisfy it have determined feeding schedules. When behavioristic psychology emerged in the United States, in the early 1900s, strict adherence to feeding schedules became a favored doctrine passed down from experts to mothers. Most authorities today recommend a more relaxed approach and advise parents to be guided by the needs and capacities of the baby rather than by set time intervals. A similar attitude prevails regarding weaning practices. Most babies in the course of infancy will have been introduced to bottle and cup feeding, or to solid foods, so that a gradual transition rather than abrupt withdrawal of breast or bottle is likely. In any case, there is no persuasive evidence that the baby's personality is affected substantially by either timing of feeding or method of weaning.

5
Toddlerhood Through the Preschool Years

The period between the end of infancy and the entry of the child into formal school comprises toddlerhood and the preschool years. Toddlerhood is usually designated as the period between eighteen months and two and a half years. The preschool years are the remaining months before the fifth birthday.

By the end of infancy the child has become a mobile, social individual. He is capable of self-directed movement; he can walk and may even run. He has begun to refine his linguistic skills into words and primitive sentences. Social interactions with the adults around him are developing, and he has begun to evince an interest in other children. He is becoming an individual, clearly distinguishable from other persons. The child of eighteen months, nevertheless, remains an "infant-child." He is still relatively helpless and dependent upon his caretakers. His ability to communicate is extremely limited, as is his capacity to explore and to understand his world.

By age five the child's body proportions, although still immature, resemble those of an adult. He no longer looks like a baby. Physical growth has been accompanied by the development of a variety of motor skills. He can use his hands and legs with a high degree of competence. He walks, runs, skips, and climbs without difficulty. The five-year-old shows marked progress in his movement away from dependency. His social world has expanded. He is able to spend several consecutive hours away from home with adults other than his parents. As his facility with language increases, his play with peers takes on a complexity that is a preview of the interpersonal relationships he will enter into later in life. By the end of this period the child is capable of a higher level of cognition, which, together with increased language skills, provides him with the tools he needs for the academic tasks of the middle years.

PHYSICAL DEVELOPMENT

The physical development of the child from the second through the fifth year of life is marked by many bodily changes. By the end of these preschool years the somewhat clumsy, bottom-heavy two-year-old will have developed into a child who has substantial mastery over his body.

Biological Changes. During toddlerhood and the preschool years, the child continues to make strides toward adulthood in both growth and appearance. Not only do his height and weight increase but his bodily proportions also change. Limbs and trunk grow rapidly to overtake the upper-body development of the first two years. The child's cerebral cortex continues to grow as new cells are added, and the brain becomes heavier. By the time the child is five years old the brain has reached 75 percent of its ultimate weight. Muscles and bones grow stronger during this period, permitting greater mastery of motor skills.

HEIGHT AND WEIGHT. Although the rapid physical growth patterns that mark the first two years of life begin to level off in toddlerhood, gains in height and weight during the preschool years are nevertheless significant. Growth data collected by the National Center for Health Statistics place the median height of three-year-old boys at 37.4 inches (95 cm) and the median weight at 33 pounds (15 kg) (26). Girls of similar age lag slightly behind boys in both height and weight. In the ensuing two years a further increase in height of about 5 to 6 inches can be anticipated in boys and girls as well as a further gain in weight of about 8 to 10 pounds. A strong correlation exists between height at preschool age and adult height. Thus, a child who is taller than average at five has a 70 percent chance of becoming a tall adult.

Baby fat is gradually reduced by about 50 percent during the preschool years, giving the child a more elongated and adult appearance. This loss of fat tissue occurring during a period of weight gain makes it appear that the child's weight has remained constant even though there is an increase of about 5 pounds a year. Muscular development, especially of the large muscles, accounts for a substantial part of the child's weight.

SKELETAL STRUCTURE. Whereas head and upper-body growth was prominent during the early years, during toddlerhood and the preschool years the growth of arms and legs accelerates. Cartilaginous portions of the skeleton continue to ossify. As the ratio of head to body size changes, the child's physique approaches adult proportions.

SPHINCTER MUSCLES. Voluntary control of the sphincter muscles that govern elimination of urine and feces does not usually occur until eighteen months and often not until the second year. Conscious control of rectal muscles is not completed until after development of the nerves that govern the ability to walk. Persistent toilet training efforts exerted before maturational readiness may place undue stress upon the child. Freud and others have theorized that punitive and guilt-producing behavior on the part of parents in this regard may lead to eventual personality problems for the child.

ENVIRONMENTAL INFLUENCES ON GROWTH. Growth during the preschool years, as at all stages, is under genetic control. Environmental forces, however, are becoming more influential through their effect on the endocrine glands involved in growth at this stage, and on the general physical health of the child. As a result, a child's growth may be accelerated or retarded by such external factors as malnutrition and illness. Inadequate intake of proteins, carbohydrates, vitamins, and minerals cannot support normal growth patterns or provide sufficient amounts of energy for the young child. Poorly nourished children do not grow at the same rate as their more fortunate agemates. The effect of poor nutrition after the second year can be reversed if the contributing causes are ameliorated early enough. Severe malnutrition during prenatal and postnatal periods, however, can permanently impair development.

Childhood illnesses can also retard growth. With renewed health, most children catch up to their normal growth; in the case of protracted illness, however, the child is sometimes unable to fulfill his full growth potential.

Expansion of Motor Skills. The eighteen- to twenty-four-month-old baby has been described as largely motor-driven. He runs around awkwardly, stopping at random to explore or examine a particular item, and then pushes on. This generalized busyness gradually gives way to more directed and efficient motor activities in the preschool years.

LOCOMOTION. The sensory motor skills of the two-year-old represent a tremendous amount of neuromuscular development. In but twenty-four months, bodily functioning which was at first limited to random reflexive movements has progressed to the point where the toddler can walk both forward and backward, as well as run. During the ensuing preschool years, the child's balance and stability improve considerably, enabling him to climb stairs in an upright position, to jump, and to turn somersaults. The preschool child becomes adept at riding a tricycle. By five years of age, the child has mastered the fundamental skills of locomotion.

USE OF ARMS AND HANDS. As the baby gains in proficiency in standing upright and walking with a steady gait, his hands and arms are freed for independent action. The toddler is able to carry things around the house and to pull and push all sorts of mechanical toys, thus demonstrating gross motor control of the arms. As he matures during the preschool years he becomes more adept manipulatively; he throws a ball with more accuracy and is able to stack and arrange blocks into complex structural designs. According to Gesell's normative studies of motor behavior, improved perceptual-motor coordination and fine motor control enable the three-year-old to hold a crayon securely and to copy a circle or horizontal line. The four-year-old is usually able to copy a cross and trace (but not copy) a diamond. He can also button his clothes. By five, most children can copy a triangle or prism and lace and unlace their shoes (11).

LATERALITY. Laterality, or the preference for using one arm, hand, or foot over the other, usually is not well established until the child's third or fourth year. By the end of the fifth year nine out of ten children in the United States have become right-handed. This does not mean that all functions are necessarily performed with the right hand; it is not unusual for a person to write and eat with the right hand and throw a ball with the left. The fact that a child is right-handed does not imply right-eye or right-foot dominance. Since we live in a dextral (right-handed) society, most children are encouraged to be right-handed. There is some indication, however, that heredity plays a role in handedness, and it is therefore wise to respect a child's preference for left-handedness when there are persistent signs of left-hand dominance.

MENTAL DEVELOPMENT

Physical changes are probably the most apparent evidence of growth in the child during toddlerhood and the preschool years. Nevertheless, as in every period of development, physical changes are accompanied by the steady growth of other characteristics and components which play a significant role in the overall adjustment and functioning of the child.

Language Development. One of the most noticeable changes in the mental development of the child from eighteen months to five years is his increased ability to understand and use language. Language involves structure, or grammar—the way in which sounds and words are put together. Language also involves meaning, or semantics—the way words, phrases, and sentences are used and the cognitive and emotional reactions they evoke.

Researchers studying the acquisition and development of language have observed similar sociolinguistic patterns in diverse cultures (18). In noting this similarity in the sequential development of language, David McNeill, a noted authority, writes, "Normal children not impaired by deafness, brain damage or other physical or psychic disorders, begin to babble at about 6 months, utter a first 'word' at 10 to 12 months, combine words at 18 to 24 months, and acquire syntax almost completely at 48 to 60 months. All children pass through such a sequence of 'milestones,' always at roughly these same ages. They do so regardless of the language they acquire, or the circumstances under which they acquire it" (19, p.1062). Children learn grammatical usage relatively quickly. Although they may omit connecting words, they know that there is a correct and an incorrect word relationship in a statement. For example, the English-speaking child says "go-bye" rather than "bye-go."

FACTORS THAT INFLUENCE LANGUAGE ACQUISITION. Although all children go through the same sequential process in acquiring language, some learn words and syntax more quickly than others. A child's genetically programmed physical development and his intellectual potential interact with the social world in which he grows up to produce his particular rate of language development.

Cultural Influences. The language form and usage employed by the adults in the child's immediate surroundings are a major factor in the child's development of language skills. Cultures, ethnic groups, and individual families all vary in the degree to which the spoken word carries meaning. In some social groups the toddler learns that body movements or single words are the usual modes of communication. In others, sentences are fully set out so that children learn to be orally articulate. Furthermore, social classes differ in the emphasis placed on informal and formal language. Thus children from lower socioeconomic groups or from strong ethnic backgrounds may experience difficulty in a formal school setting because the language with which they are most familiar differs from the language used by the teacher. Consequently, family living styles, social class, and cultural background significantly influence the way children learn language and how they use it.

Maturation. Language acquisition unfolds with biological maturation. Commenting on the findings of some crucial similarities in the sequence of language development in young children throughout the world, McNeill writes: "Such massive regularities of development remind one more of the maturation of a physical process, say walking, than of a process of education, say reading. One might even say that children cannot help learning a language, whereas they can easily avoid learning to read" (19, p. 1062). McNeill points out, however, that language must nevertheless be learned. Children who are deaf from birth or who, for some other reason, have not been exposed to language do not learn to speak although they vocalize as infants.

Cognitive Ability. Intellectual or cognitive ability has some effect on language acquisition. For the developing child, language is more than a means of communication—it is a vehicle for ordering the world as it unfolds. As a child's cognitive ability increases, so does his language ability.

Theoreticians hold different points of view on the relationship between language and thought (18). Some suggest that language is merely thought put into words, that cognition directs language development. To support their position, they cite evidence that infants are capable of preverbal thinking, and the ability of some deaf children with limited language facility to solve cognitive problems. Others hold the opposite—that language development determines cognitive ability. Principal among the latter theoreticians is Benjamin Lee Whorf, a linguist who studied languages in different cultures. According to the *Whorfian hypothesis,* language determines and restricts thought (6). In effect, ideas cannot go beyond the words that our culture imposes upon us. The words we learn shape our thinking and thus our behavior, confining both activities within the accepted norms of our society and culture. We conceive the unknown in terms of the known, according to Whorf, and define it with words used to describe the known. Thus, by definition, it is impossible to conceive of the inconceivable. Mythical gods and science fiction characters and situations must be described in words which are familiar and which place the idea into existing linguistic frameworks.

THEORIES OF LANGUAGE ACQUISITION. There is as much difference of opinion about how we acquire language as about its relationship to thought. Among the principal theoreticians here are B. F. Skinner (21) and Noam Chomsky (7).

Skinner and Reinforcement Theory. B. F. Skinner theorized that the learning of language follows the accepted pattern of operant conditioning through selective reinforcement. The baby utters random sounds which are selectively reinforced by mother, father, and others. When the child utters a sound resembling one that has meaning to his parents, they reward him with a smile or some other form of encouragement. The sounds "ma-ma" or "da-da," for example, evoke favorable reactions from English-speaking parents. These sounds are then integrated into the words "Mama" and "Daddy." According to Skinnerian theory, the entire process of language acquisition is one of selective reinforcement of sounds and sound combinations. The child learns that the sound "up" results in his being picked up; "ball" is rewarded with a ball; whereas "ta" may evoke nothing more than a questioning frown.

Although imitation and learning are involved, the child's early speech cannot be explained on these grounds alone. Children understand more than they can articulate; they speak in sentences that they have never heard before; they spontaneously use words that have not been taught to them. The adults around them usually speak in more or less correct linguistic form, yet children alter linguistic patterns while retaining meaning and syntax. For example, mother may say to father: "She wants a glass of milk," referring to their daughter and spoken in front of her. The daughter says, "Her want milk," referring to her doll or to herself.

Chomsky's Theory. In an approach diametrically opposed to that of operant conditioning, Noam Chomsky advances the theory that children possess an inborn ability to learn the language of their society. Chomsky refers to this innate capacity or skill as the Language Acquisition Device (LAD). LAD is obviously not a device in the literal sense but rather a set of neurological mechanisms, genetically directed, which are triggered into operation by the language patterns to which the child is exposed. As children listen to themselves and to others, they utilize the LAD to formulate increasingly precise rules of grammar and then to articulate meaningful sounds, words, phrases, and sentences. Although the young child's language is at first a rough approximation of the language of his society, the basic rules of grammar are evident even in the earliest meaningful combination of words. This, according to Chomsky, indicates the existence of the LAD. Chomsky further develops his theory by distinguishing between the *surface structure* of language, the ways in which languages differ from one another, and the *deep structure,* the universalities existing in all languages, including a grammatical form or set of rules and linguistic designations. As McNeill explains it, "The deep structure of a sentence is associated with meaning and the surface structure with sound" (19, p. 1086). Deep structures are converted into surface structures by a set of transformational rules.

GRADUAL INCREASE IN LANGUAGE SKILLS. Whatever the explanation for language acquisition, by four years of age the child speaks with relative facility. There have been, however, many intervening steps between the first words of infancy and the complex sentences of the preschool period.

The baby's first comprehensible sounds are known as *phonemes.* Phonemes have been defined as the smallest unit of sound that conveys meaning. There are about forty-five phonemes in the English language, including vowels and consonants. The sounds of *b, p, t,* and *e* are examples of phonemes. These sounds are not exactly the same as alphabetical letters; the sound of the alphabetical *b,* or "bee," for example, can vary from "bu" as in "but" to the sound heard in "web."

As the baby's skill in vocalization increases, phonemes are combined to produce *morphemes,* which are the basic linguistic elements of meaning. Morphemes are sounds which cannot be divided or broken up without a change in meaning. They can be words such as "bed" and "dog"; they can also be parts of words such as prefixes and suffixes; or they can be combinations of sounds which designate plurality or tenses.

During the period of babbling and expressive vocalizations, the baby gradually begins to use more morphemes to form words. First words usually appear in mid-infancy. They are generally referred to as *holophrases* because they are used by the child as substitutes for complete sentences. The spoken word "car" may mean "I want to go for a ride in the car" or "I hear a car" or have any of a number of complex meanings. According to one study (22), the child's vocabulary gradually expands to about 22 words at eighteen months, then increases rapidly to about 272 words by age two. Although other studies show variations in these numbers, it is clear that children's spoken vocabulary increases with age. Authorities agree that children understand more words than they use, that is, they acquire passive, or receptive, language along with active language. During the period between eighteen months and two years of age the child not only acquires a great many words but begins to communicate by combining words into two-word statements, thereby making his meaning clearer. This marks a major step in language development.

During this stage, the child also begins to demonstrate an understanding of grammatical rules. There is, however, some disagreement on whether the child is actually applying rudimentary understanding of syntactic rules or simply combining words for purposes of expression, since grammatical usage at this early age would probably be beyond his conceptual grasp.

The child's vocabulary continues to increase so that by age three to four he is likely to have a speaking knowledge of 1,500 words and by five years, 2,000 words. At first, words are combined in what is termed *telegraphic speech*. Such speech resembles a telegram in that a minimum of words are used to convey the message. Gradually the sentences increase in length, and prepositions, articles, and other grammatical units are added.

The timing of language development varies from child to child. One measure of the level of linguistic development of children in the early years has been formulated by Roger Brown (3), who studied the progress of three children. First he computed the average number of morphemes in each child's utterance, which he called the *mean length of utterance,* or MLU. Then he divided language development into five stages according to MLU levels. He found that each child went through each stage sequentially, but at slightly different ages (4). One child reached stage two (2.0 to 2.5 MLU) at about twenty months of age, stage three (2.5 to 3.0 MLU) at about twenty-two months, stage four (3.0 to 3.75 MLU) at about twenty-three months, and stage five (3.75 to 4.5 and beyond) at about twenty-five to twenty-six months. In contrast, another child was about twenty-nine months old when she reached stage one, and forty-two months when she achieved stage five.

Between the ages of fifteen months and five years, not only do children learn more and more words, they also communicate with increasingly complex grammatical sentences and forms. The interrogatory form is an early acquisition, although it may consist only of a rising inflection at the end of such a two-word elision as "aw gone." In time the child develops facility with this grammatical form, and by the age of five can ask questions properly. By this time he will also have learned the basic rules of syntax. Although he still retains childish phraseology, he displays an extensive vocabulary while his understanding of language, as noted previously, is even greater.

INFLUENCES AFFECTING THE RATE OF LANGUAGE DEVELOPMENT. Although language development is complex and not fully understood, it is apparent that biological and social factors are influential in determining how that process evolves in each child.

Biological Factors. Piaget and others subscribe to the view that innate biological factors underlie the pace at which children develop language facility. Children in all parts of the world, in a multitude of different language systems, appear to follow the same basic progression in learning language. Furthermore, in each culture some children pass linguistic milestones earlier than others. Thus, although all children progress through similar stages cross-culturally, they vary in their rate of progression.

Since intellectual ability is rooted in the biological organism and is therefore influenced by the maturational process, intellect also plays a role in language development. The more intelligent the child, the quicker he learns to ascribe meaning to sounds. The brighter child develops a larger vocabulary in a shorter time; he uses that vocabulary in more complex sentence structures and at an earlier stage, and he is thus more facile and skilled with language quantitatively and qualitatively. Further possible corroboration of the view that the rate and nature of language development are genetically programed is demonstrated by the high correlation between language ability and mental ability as measured by intelligence tests. This evidence, however, must be viewed with caution, since the validity of intelligence testing has been seriously questioned. Since intelligence tests are based to a large extent on verbal-language skills, it is to be expected that children who excel in language will perform better in linguistically based tests than children who are slow in developing language skills.

Social Class. Many studies point out variances in all aspects of language skill between children of different social classes. Children of middle- and upper-class families are generally ahead of their peers with lower socioeconomic backgrounds, in vocabulary size, in length of sentence structure, and in verbal curiosity. This is primarily because their parents tend to be highly verbal.

An English educational sociologist, Basil Bernstein, suggests that parents of different social classes transmit language to their children through a form of coding (2). He found that lower socioeconomic parents speak in *restricted language codes*. They make grammatically simple statements in which explanations are minimal or omitted entirely. Their communication is accomplished through a combination of expressions, postures, and gestures, as well as through simplified verbalizations. Children growing up in such families learn to "read" meanings from a variety of contextual and behavioral cues, and thus rely less on linguistic skills. Middle- and upper-class parents tend to communicate in *elaborated language codes* which involve greater reliance on words and verbal expressions, explanations, and specific word meanings. Their children consequently develop greater skills in the use of complex sentence structure in order to convey and receive meaning. Linguistic authorities differ as to the superiority of one or the other of these approaches to language development, but there is general agreement that children in the United States who speak in restricted code language, or, to use another term, in nonstandard English, use complex grammatical forms, even though the surface structure of their speech may seem simplistic.

USES OF LANGUAGE. Language serves a variety of purposes:

In Communication. Language is primarily a vehicle of communication. It is used in schools, in books, at work, and in a myriad of daily activities.

As a Tool in Thinking and Learning. Words, phrases, and sentences are facilitators in the process of labeling, conceptualizing, and understanding ideas and phenomena.

As a Source of Pleasure. The young child "plays" with the sound of a word that intrigues him; the sound rather than its meaning is pleasurable. Later he will "play" with a word because of its meaning. Much as the baby repeatedly goes up and down stairs, or bangs pots and pans, he pronounces a word over and over again. More refined examples of this use of language are found in the poetic form and in drama, in which appreciation derives from the sound and cadence of the words.

As a Tool in Orientation. Young children use words (I, me, mine) as part of the process of ego development in differentiating the self from the nonself (you, it, that). Language is used to form spatial orientations (here, there) and to designate time intervals (now, tomorrow, nine o'clock in the morning).

As a Controller of Behavior. In the Whorfian hypothesis, discussed previously, there is the suggestion that language serves as a controller of behavior. Words become mediators between impulse or thought and action. The word "no," said by a child to himself, stops the impulse to engage in an unacceptable act.

As a Vehicle of Socialization. The Piagetian view that children do not use speech in a social sense (i.e., they are unable to consider the points of view of others) until seven or eight years of age has been disputed. Some authorities see speech as a social force in children as young as three or four. In any case, it is important to note that language development affects the amount, nature, and quality of social intercourse among children.

Cognition. From eighteen months to five years the child makes rapid progress in developing cognitive skills. He shifts from dealing primarily with the concrete and tangible to the use of mental representations, such as images and symbols. By the time he leaves the preschool years he will have begun to use relatively simple concepts and will have established rules of thinking that lead him to a better understanding of his world and enable him to generate ideas.

Cognitive development is closely interwoven with the physical, neurological, social, and psychological aspects of total development. The extent and quality of each child's knowledge and thought processes are affected by his particular physical makeup, his family relationships, his social background, and his reservoir of experiences.

UNITS OF COGNITION. The word "cognition" encompasses the fundamental units of knowing and thinking and the processes by which these units are used. The units of cognition are schemata, images, symbols, concepts, and rules.

Schemata. The infant's first mental representations evolve through the schema, a blueprintlike view of his experiences (already discussed in Chapter 4).

Images. Images first occur at about two years of age when the child begins to recall in more specific representational form that which he has encountered. The image is probably visual, although, as language skills grow, the child may add linguistic elaborations. Jerome Bruner, who, like Piaget, has described stages of cognitive development, calls this period the *ikonic representation* stage because it is essentially visual. According to Bruner, this is a major type of mental activity throughout the early years (5).

Symbols. The symbol is not as much a representation of an object or an event as an abstraction which stands for something. The child learns gradually that the picture he sees in a book represents a real object and, later, that the word he reads (e.g., "car" or "ball") stands for a real car or ball. Similarly, the word "Daddy" is a symbol that stands for or signifies the actual father. By the time he is five years of age, the child has developed a relatively high degree of skill in recognizing and using symbols. He has learned that a picture of red flames means fire, that arrows on a street sign mean direction, and that the movement of the hands on a clock represent the passage of time.

By his use of images and symbols, the child is able to abstract and carry into the future many aspects of his world and his experiences. He can reexperience mentally; he can consider, enjoy, or modify what he has encountered in the past. In effect, he is beginning to think.

Concepts. As he matures and experiences many new situations, the child recognizes that some objects, people, things, and events fit together while others do not. These elements may have some characteristics in common and others which are different. For example, both dogs and cats walk on four legs and have fur, but dogs bark while cats mew. Gradually the child is able to form higher-level abstractions. The very young child can recognize a toy truck, then he recognizes the sound of the word "truck" as a representation of the toy truck. A greater representational distance is reached when the child recognizes that the toy truck represents the real truck. An even greater form of abstraction is achieved when the symbol, the written word "truck," is recognized as signifying and thus bearing an equivalence to the toy truck, the sound of the word "truck," and the real truck. A yet higher level of abstractive ability occurs when a blueprint is understood to stand for a real house, although there is no pictorial relationship between the lines on the blueprint and the bricks and wood of the house.

As the child's ability to abstract, generalize, and increase the distance between the immediate object and its representation grows, he begins to form and use concepts. A *concept* is an abstraction or idea of a group of related schemata, images, and symbols related to concrete and specific events, people, or things. A musical note is a symbol that stands for a specific individual musical sound. The concept of music is a high-level generalization that includes many musical notes in many contexts. Concepts are ideas; they do not refer to the specific and concrete, as do symbols. They deal with groupings, categories, and classifications, or equivalencies from which the concept is derived.

Rules. Rules are relationships between concepts. By means of rules, children recognize, establish, utilize, and manipulate relationships. Thus, the relationship between the concept of coldness and the winter may lead to expectancy of snow. Rules are sometimes categorized as formal or informal, depending upon whether the relationship is fixed or variable. Mathematical relationships are subsumed under *formal rules.* The sum of the three angles of any triangle is 180 degrees. Relationships relating to certain scientific principles come under the category of formal rules. Water freezes at 0 degrees Celsius or 32 degrees Fahrenheit. *Informal rules* are those applying to relationships which vary with changing circumstances or inconstant factors. "Summer is hot, and winter is cold" exemplifies an informal rule. The relationship may or may not apply, depending upon a particular summer or winter, a specific day, or individual interpretations of hot and cold. Formal or informal rules permit the organization of thought into logical sequences.

EMERGENCE OF UNITS OF COGNITION. It is difficult to present a clear-cut developmental timetable for the emergence of the units of cognition because the presence of imagery or of concepts in very young children is not obvious and must be inferred. Nevertheless, maturation and experience appear to play significant roles in the timing of the functional presence of these fundamental elements of thought. As the child's capacity to attend, perceive with discrimination, store, and retrieve information increases, so does his capacity to use these functions in learning higher-level skills. The more the child is exposed to experience and learning, the better he can utilize the higher-level skills available to him. As these skills develop and function in language growth, the use of symbols, concepts, and rules is correspondingly more evident. Thus, cognitive development between eighteen months and five years is characterized by the increasing refinement of earlier tools of cognition (perception, language, and so forth) and by the emergence of complex functions which become integrated into the cognitive structure. Throughout, this process is intimately related in its functional levels to the overall development of the child. The younger and less socially experienced the child, the more rudimentary the cognitive functions; the older and more socially exposed the child, the more complex is the thinking process.

Although the development of symbolic representation is often associated with the middle years of childhood, much younger children use symbols and manifest the presence of concepts. Such ideas as "good," "bad," or "nice," though vague and certainly fluctuating in definition, are concepts commonly encountered in two-year-olds and appear frequently in the moral judgments of four- and five-year-old children.

PIAGET'S PREOPERATIONAL STAGE. Piaget calls the period from approximately two to seven years of age the preoperational stage of intellectual development. In this period children use *preconcepts,* concepts that are incomplete. Piaget points out that preoperational children can classify and organize but in a rudimentary fashion. Reasoning and thinking are limited. For example, children in this stage don't realize that changes in shape or color do not necessarily mean that the essential nature of an object has changed (conservation). They do, however, exhibit mental activity that is a precursor of higher levels of conceptual thinking. In effect, Piaget considers the period from two years to seven years as a time of getting ready for adult thought. The closer the child approaches seven years of age and the next stage of concrete operations, the more signs he will show of higher-level cognitive processes.

COGNITIVE DEPRIVATION AND ENRICHMENT. Early life experiences have a profound effect on cognitive development. Institutionalized infants living in situations of emotional and physical deprivation, according to many investigators, suffer trauma that retards mental growth (24). Appropriate and opportune intervention, however, may help many of these children recover lost ground. Children with intellectually impoverished backgrounds may show low academic achievement and poor intelligence test scores.

In an attempt to provide equal educational opportunities to all children in the United States, and particularly to counteract the lack of intellectual stimulation in the backgrounds of the children of poor families, a number of childhood programs have been devised and set up. Chief among them is Project Head Start, a federally funded program established in the 1960s as part of President Lyndon Johnson's war on poverty. This compensatory educational program was expected to increase IQ levels and better prepare children for elementary school education. Children in the program were also expected to receive training in the kinds of skills that would lead to future social competence. In some situations, teachers went into homes and trained children in cognitive and affective tasks. In others, children were brought to specially enriched educational centers. Efforts were also made to help parents learn child-care and teaching techniques. Some programs throughout the country were specific in content, whereas others were more milieu-oriented. In all instances the training started well before the usual age for entrance into elementary school. When, in 1967, the federal government made carefully controlled studies of the effectiveness of Head Start (8), it was found that the enrichment provided by the preschool programs did not significantly raise the achievement levels of the participants above those of children of similar backgrounds who were not involved in the programs. Some gains in academic areas were observed in some programs. Some children seemed to have derived some benefits in nonacademic aspects of development. But the high hopes that had given rise to the Head Start compensatory education program seemed unrealized. The report of the United States Commission on Civil

Rights which undertook the evaluation has not, however, been universally accepted. Some critics attribute the lack of success to the poor design of many of the programs. Others point out the need to intervene on a broader level than the traditional preschool curriculum, which formed the core of most of the programs (20, 25).

Strong evidence that well-conceived enrichment programs can produce significant and lasting effects is found in reports on the "Milwaukee Project" (25), a comprehensive intervention program directed by Rick Heber of the University of Wisconsin. In this project, an experimental group of children and their intellectually limited mothers, living in economically depressed areas, received intensive training and guidance, at first in their own homes and later in educational centers. The training started in infancy with a teacher assigned to each child. The teacher assumed full responsibility for working with the individual child five days a week, seven hours a day, until the child entered the first grade at the age of six years. The training extended into all areas of development—physical, intellectual, social, and emotional. Cognitive and language skills were emphasized in the training plan. Since the 1960s, when the program started, the experimental group has experienced consistently more advanced development in cognitive areas, school achievement, and intelligence test scores than children in the control group.

Further support for the effectiveness of enrichment programs is found in a report presented by Francis Palmer to the President's Commission on Mental Health in July 1977 (20). In this paper, Palmer analyzed the results of ten early-childhood intervention programs involving six hundred children in experimental and control groups. The statistics marshaled by Palmer to support his argument for intervention include:

1. Percent of children in each group who have been retained in grade in school
2. Percent in special education classes
3. Reading achievement
4. Arithmetic achievement
5. Norm-referenced tests of general intelligence
6. Responses of parents and children to the program

Palmer concludes that an examination of these studies "provides hard evidence that a variety of early interventions can improve the child's scholastic performance in the elementary grades" (20, p. 70).

These various inconsistent results suggest that further research into the benefits of compensatory education is needed. It may well be that factors which have not as yet been considered have a stronger influence on whether a child benefits from a compensatory program than does the method or content of the program utilized. In a recent study, for example, Kagan, Kearsley, and Zelazo explored the effects of day-care programs on infants from 3.5 to 29 months who were enrolled in a group day-care center five days a week from 8:30 A.M. until 4:00 P.M. (16). These children were compared with a matched group who lived at home. The findings indicated that: "Attendance at a day-care center staffed by conscientious and nurturant adults during the first 2.5 years does seem to sculpt a psychological profile very different from the one created by total home rearing." The most significant conclusion of the authors is that "the effects of the home appear to have a salience that is not easily altered by the group-care context. The family has a mysterious power . . ." (16, p. 139). Such conclusions suggest that the home, the mother, her attitudes, education, and degree of involvement with the child, and the importance of these influences in the cognitive domain may be more significant than an enrichment program provided outside the home. The success of such projects as the Milwaukee Project and the failure of other programs rich in content but lacking in the most significant of focus—the home—may thus be explained. However, more study is obviously needed in this area.

PERSONALITY DEVELOPMENT

Many facets of development are combined in that characteristic termed personality. Each individual is a composite of all that has gone into his development, physical and mental. The early years of life are particularly formative. It is at this time that the child begins to sense and test out his autonomy, achieving the beginning steps of independence. He begins to form his concept of self, establish his sexual identification, and develop qualities of aggressiveness and altruism. By the time the child enters school, he is a distinct individual.

Stages of Personality Development. The period from eighteen months through five years of age encompasses a great deal in terms of personality development. Both Erikson and Freud recognized distinct stages that correspond to toddlerhood and the preschool period.

TODDLERHOOD. For Erikson the toddler has developed basic trust and is now confronted with the task of becoming more independent. For Freud, the toddler passes from the oral to the anal stages.

Erikson's Stage of Autonomy. Erikson highlights the crisis of this age as the choice between autonomy or shame and doubt. In Eriksonian theory, the toddler's growing sense of himself as a competent and independent human being determines his future ability to adjust to the world around him. Self-determination, as a personality trait, depends upon many factors, but generally in Western society it rests upon the parents' responses to the child's acquisition and use of various skills. The child exercises his new abilities by behaviors which are not always sanctioned by parents. For example, he may test out his teeth by chewing the crib, or his eye-hand coordination by pushing a glass of milk to the floor. The manner in which parents handle such explorations encourages or discourages growth toward autonomy. At one end of Erikson's developmental continuum is the child who is willing to take risks because he knows he is loved and relatively secure. As he strives to become more autonomous, the toddler manifests the negativism which has given this period the title "the 'No' stage." Yet in the next moment he can be most appealing and accommodating, feeling safe to be both assertive and acquiescent. At the other extreme of Erikson's continuum is the child of overprotective, overindulgent, or overly harsh parents who develops a feeling of doubt about his competence and a sense of shame about himself and his normal strivings.

Erikson, like Freud, associates later-life personality traits with toilet-training management. For the young child, says Erikson, the ability to control excretory functions is significant in the context of his growing competence and autonomy. He is, to some extent, the master of this physical function and it is up to him to conform to social expectations. Parents who provide nonpunitive toilet training convey their love for their child, even when he has temporary lapses, and show their confidence in his eventual ability to achieve complete control. Lack of understanding and impatience in toilet training, on the other hand, tend to make the child feel incapable of ever achieving complete control. This kind of uncertainty is then generalized to such other developmental tasks as talking, dressing, and socialization. The child who, either directly or indirectly, is made to feel ashamed of his incontinence is likely to develop feelings of doubt and shame about himself rather than a sense of competence and autonomy.

Freud's Anal Stage. In Freudian theory, need satisfaction shifts from one body area to another as the child passes through the stages of development. In toddlerhood the anal area becomes the focus of gratification. Freud sees the interaction between parent and child during the bowel-training period as a primary source of a variety of later personality characteristics.

The child's excretory functions become the focus of parental concern, pride, and displeasure, and may lead to emphasis on restraint and control in bowel training. Freud believes that through the medium of toilet training, the child develops attitudes toward excrement which are later generalized to other dimensions of life and behavior. The concept of dirty, for example, may be inappropriately extended to include sex. The manner in which toilet training is handled also affects the child's feelings about compliance with parents' wishes. These feelings may then be generalized to other life circumstances—compliance with or defiance of authority figures such as teachers and policemen.

Freud holds that unduly harsh toilet-training methods may cause emotional traumas that result in less than satisfactory resolution of the developmental needs and conflicts of this period. When this happens, the child is said to have become fixated at the anal stage. Such a child may grow up to be excessively moralistic, overly concerned with possessions, or obsessively orderly.

PRESCHOOL PERIOD. The years following toddlerhood, through age five, have important personality implications for both Erikson and Freud.

Erikson's Stage of Initiative. In Eriksonian terms, the child at three or four is faced with the developmental issue of initiative versus guilt. As a psychosocial stage theorist, Erikson understands developmental resolutions in childhood in terms of the child's interactions with the social world. The thrust toward autonomy in the preschool years becomes the basis for the satisfaction of a growing curiosity. The child wishes to know, and thus he undertakes to explore the physical and social world in which he lives. Because this period is one in which the child's conscience or superego is developing, Erikson sees the child incorporating his new-found skills into a beginning moral system. Failure to achieve this positive resolution of the developmental steps of this stage leads to low self-esteem, a lack of confidence, and a fear of trying, because of fear of failure. The overall result is a rigid superego and eventual feelings of excessive and disabling guilt.

Freud's Phallic Stage. In Freud's scheme, the bodily focus for both boys and girls shifts from the anal to the genital area. The use of the term "phallic" at this stage is based on the view that the penis, or the lack of it, is of major concern. This concern is interwoven with the child's fantasized romantic relationship with the parent of the opposite sex. It leads to the Oedipal conflict and a variety of anxieties and emotions that are extremely upsetting to the child. The manner in which these conflicts and developmental issues are resolved determines, in great part, the future success or failure of the individual's adult sexual relationships and psychosexual identifications.

Self-Awareness. The infant appears to have no awareness of himself as a separate entity. As he grows physiologically, however, and begins to differentiate and attach meanings to various objects, people, and experiences, he gradually becomes aware of his own individuality.

By two years of age toddlers are conscious of their separateness. However, unity of self is not always clear—that is, at times they do not seem to realize that their various parts and attributes all constitute a single whole person. In one study, children were found to have "localized" themselves in various parts of their bodies (14). One child, for example, identified himself with his head, another with her arm. By age five, most children have a clear and integrated body image.

Self-Concept. The self-concept is an internalized image which each person has of himself, in addition to his personal evaluation of his separate characteristics. It is comprised of strengths and limitations, appearance, physique, intellect, behavior, and achievement.

THE IMPORTANCE OF SELF-CONCEPT. An individual's evaluation of himself influences many aspects of his behavior. A child who does not believe he can succeed will be less likely to try than one who is self-confident, whether the task is feeding himself, learning to talk, riding a bicycle, or making friends. The way the child sees himself governs how he feels and how he will act. Feelings of being pretty or handsome, wanted, adept, cute, or bright foster satisfaction, contentment, and happiness. Seeing oneself as ugly, annoying, inept, or stupid leads to moroseness, depression, or anger. The development of a positive self-image should thus be a major goal in child rearing.

DETERMINANTS OF SELF-CONCEPT. Many factors contribute to the formation of a child's image of himself. Among these are the assessments and influence of his family members, his peers, and other significant people, and the successes and failures of his daily life.

Influence of People. Inasmuch as the child's parents and his immediate family are the primary sources of need satisfaction and protection in infancy and early childhood, they naturally serve as the most significant influence in the shaping of the child's self-image during those periods. They continually transmit messages to the child of a judgmental nature. "You are a darling"; "You are Daddy's pretty girl"; "Look how big you're getting"; "My goodness, you're clumsy." Such evaluative statements along with the attitudes inherent in them become the basis for a self-concept that persists throughout life. As he grows older a child tends selectively to accept feedback from the environment that is consistent with his own assessment of himself, and to block out that which he feels does not fit. Believing himself to be clumsy, for instance, a child may accept dropping and breaking a dish as proof of his clumsiness rather than recognizing that the dish was slippery or that dishes may be carelessly dropped by anyone. A child's perceived self-image is not necessarily what he is really like. He may feel ugly or stupid when he is in fact good-looking and intelligent. The greater the discrepancy between a child's perception of himself and how he is perceived by others, the greater the possibility that the child will experience adjustment difficulties.

As the child moves out of the family orbit, his peers, preschool teachers, and other nonfamily adults influence his evolving self-concept. In general, the greater the significance of the person, and the more regular the contact, the greater the impact on the self-image. Children with whom the preschooler associates every day and teachers to whom he is attached and sees five days a week are usually more influential in shaping the self-concept than casual acquaintances.

Influences of Experiences. Contributing significantly to the child's developing self-image are actual experiences. If, for example, the preschooler finds himself consistently able to climb a jungle gym more quickly than other children, he soon incorporates that skill and other motor skills into his image of himself as a physically adept child. If, however, he is consistently slower than his peers, his self-image will reflect his lack of success. Personal experiences shape the self-concept as part of an ongoing self-evaluative process by which the individual constantly measures himself against others.

The self-image may be established early in a child's development but remains open to modification with the impact of later life experiences and influential relationships. Social-class membership and socioeconomic status further influence a child's self-concept.

Emotions in Personality Development. The emotions of the toddler and preschool child are limited by inexperience and incomplete knowledge of the world. Primitive and irrational fears and anxieties, anger, hostility, and aggression may thus be disproportionate and inappropriate. The content and expression of these emotions are significantly interwoven with the process of personality development. Behavioral control, limited at age two, gradually becomes more refined and selective.

FEARS. From the infant's reactions to certain stimuli, psychologists have inferred the presence of fear at an early age. Very young infants make avoidance responses to approaching objects. At about six or seven months of age, babies show fear of strangers. These reactions, among others, indicate that humans are constitutionally equipped with a variety of protective responses which assist in survival. Nevertheless, many fears are not innate but are learned. Jersild and Holmes have found that some fears common before age two gradually decline in intensity and usually disappear by age five (15). Among these are fearful reactions to noise, strange objects and people, loss of physical support, and fear of being left alone. Other fears, however, take their place. These are fears associated with imaginary creatures and dark rooms, or fears of specific dangers such as fire or drowning.

Because young children cannot readily articulate their concerns, the causes of fear arousal are not easily explained. It seems likely, however, that many fears derive from perceived threats stemming from the child's inadequate fund of knowledge. Fear of being flushed down the toilet is a typical irrational fear. The preschooler's inability to fully differentiate between dreams and reality is another cause of fear in childhood. Thus the monster of a nightmare, a caged animal, or a leashed dog may arouse similar fear responses. As experience and knowledge increase, some previously frightening phenomena lose their threat potential. Conversely, increased knowledge of the environment alerts children to ever-present dangers that threaten their lives and thus creates new fears which are more reality-based. Fear of death is an example of such an apprehension. Fears stemming from fantasy, however, continue well into middle childhood.

Fears are often aroused and intensified by inadvertent comments, admonitions, and actions of parents and others. Such comments as "You'd better hang on to me or you'll get lost" or "If you do that again, the policeman will come" can create fears. Children also reflect fears they detect in their parents.

ANXIETY. Differentiation is made between fear and anxiety. As Gaylin points out, anxiety is a component of the generic emotion, fear. "Fear tends to be direct, object or event oriented, specific, and conscious. When we feel anxious, it is usually vague, indirect, with no particular source, and more unconsciously oriented" (10). Fear is considered externally based, whereas anxiety is subjective and psychological in nature. Fine distinctions between fear and anxiety are not always discernible in the emotions of young children. Their lack of experience and their tendency to confuse fantasy with reality often produce similar responses to both emotions. Both fear and anxiety have physiological correlates, but as the child matures, his ability to recognize and understand fear-producing stimuli increases. Anxiety, however, being subjective and psychologically based, is linked to the child's psychological stability rather than to the degree of rational understanding attained.

AGGRESSION AND HOSTILITY. Aggression in childhood is considered by some authorities to stem from feelings of hostility. Others view the aggressive act as a form of assertiveness derived from curiosity or from a naturally active disposition. Thus a child in a play group may monopolize the sandbox, oblivious to the wishes or needs of other children. He is neither angry nor hostile; he is assertive, and in that sense aggressive. On the other hand, a child actively defending his claim to the sandbox may generate anger which may then lead to an aggressive act of hostility, such as punching.

Ways of Expressing Aggression. In toddlerhood, the child has relatively few ways of expressing aggression and hostility. He can do little more than yell, hit, or bite. As he progresses through the years to age five, he learns other ways of expressing these feelings and develops a higher degree of control. Passive-aggressive acts of defiance and anger are adopted. Enuresis, or bed-wetting, is often associated with passive-aggressive personality traits. The passive-aggressive act is indirect, and the intent to be hostile or aggressive is psychologically denied by the child. He may be unaware that he is expressing anger toward parents. The older the child, the more likely he is to rely on verbal and symbolic modes of expression.

Origins of Aggression. Many explanations have been proffered to account for aggression in children (13). One theory correlates degree of aggression with *activity levels*. It suggests that everyone has a genetically determined activity pace in the range from hypotonic (very slow) to hypertonic (very fast). A child with a low activity level born into a high-activity family is under steady pressure to move more quickly. Such a child may feel resentful and use the activity level as a vehicle for the expression of his anger. He may deliberately dawdle. Parents who accept individual differences in their children encourage greater self-acceptance; the result is less anger and aggression.

Another explanation, called the frustration-aggression hypothesis, attributes aggression to *frustration*. When a child is thwarted in some way he will react aggressively. Although this thesis is supported by many studies, it does not account for all cases. Frustration may lead to behavior other than aggression, such as withdrawal, and aggression may occur in the apparent absence of frustration.

Most theories of aggression recognize that *social learning* is involved in the aggressive response (9). The child learns to be more or less aggressive because his parents and peers directly or indirectly, deliberately or inadvertently, encourage or disapprove of aggressive behavior. Some theoreticians believe that aggressive behavior is an assumed characteristic which develops through *imitation* of significant models, especially parents. The parent who punishes the child in a harsh manner fosters aggression, whereas the parent who is firm but not punitive becomes a model for nonaggressive behavior. Inconsistent management leads to aggressive behavior in some children but not in others.

Boys, on the whole, are more overtly aggressive than girls. One explanation that has been offered is that they are directly or indirectly encouraged in this direction by parents who follow stereotypes that equate aggressivity with masculinity. Other authorities believe that genetic programming via sex hormones acting on the early development of different parts of the brain accounts for a good part of the difference in aggression and rough-and-tumble play between boys and girls, and for other behavioral differences as well. Considerable research is going on at present to obtain more information on the causes of male-female differences in behavior (17).

Psychosexual Identification. Whereas external anatomical differences in the male and female body are clearly observable and definable, psychological differences are not. Children learn what it is to be male or female in their culture, then fit themselves into that definition (1). As cultural definitions and stereotypes change, a greater variety of expressions of psychosexuality become socially acceptable.

Most American children develop a basic sex role identity by six or seven years of age. This identity is determined to a large extent by cultural expectations transmitted to the child by his parents and his social environment. The way a child is dressed, is expected to behave, and is encouraged or discouraged to feel transmits the psychosexual stereotype. In the past (and to some degree even in the present) American parents dressed boys in blue and girls in pink; boys in pants, girls in skirts. Although change in social stereotypes has been accelerating, most parents still train boys to be self-reliant and independent, and foster a nurturing role in girls.

In the majority of children sexual identity corresponds to biological sex. Nevertheless, some children feel uncomfortable with their biological maleness or femaleness. They feel more at ease in activities and with behavior culturally expected of the opposite sex. Thus, some boys may manifest more feminine-type characteristics and some girls may reveal masculine-type qualities. Discomfort with sex-role expectations is seen clearly in homosexuality: males who respond sexually to other men and females who respond sexually to other women. An extreme expression of sexual misidentity is the rejection of biological gender by transsexuals who change their sex through surgery and hormonal intervention.

THE OEDIPAL PERIOD. Sex-role identification, according to Freudian theory, is a result of the resolution of the *Oedipal conflict*. Freud said that the full realization of anatomical differences creates intense reaction in boys and girls: *castration anxiety* in the boy who unconsciously relates the girl's lack of a penis to retaliatory punishment for harboring forbidden incestuous thoughts, and in girls, *penis envy*, a feeling of having been deprived. Through a complex psychological process, according to this theory, boys and girls resolve their conflicts and anxieties in a healthy direction by identifying with the parent of the same sex, adopting the sex-typed attitudes and values of that parent, and accepting themselves as male and female.

LEARNING AND MODELING. Other theoreticians stress the roles of learning and modeling in psychosexual identification. In the *learning* approach, parents are seen as consistently reinforcing desired behavior and attitudes in children by a variety of tangible and intangible rewards. Because parents want their children to grow into men and women who will meet the expectations of society, they reward sex-appropriate behavior and punish or discourage deviations. As a result, the child, in time, reflects the sex-role identification fostered by parents and approved by society. From the *modeling* point of view, children learn to define themselves psychosexually by modeling themselves after the same-sex parent. The son begins to fit himself into the model of his father, the male he knows best. Simultaneously, the teaching-learning process, in which desirable sex-appropriate characteristics are reinforced, gives the modeling process added impetus. A mother refers to her son as a boy and indicates clearly that he will become a man; she may call him "my little man." The father refers to a boy as "son," another variant of boy and man. The child soon internalizes a composite of reinforced attributes and parent-model characteristics. The advocates of this position go on to say that children identify more readily with the same-sex parent if that parent is nurturant and affectionate.

THE ROLE OF COGNITION. Another point of view, espoused by Lawrence Kohlberg, explains psychosexual identification in broader and more general terms than reinforcement or conditioned learning. Kohlberg believes that sex-typing and role behavior are related to growth of cognitive capacity: the child observes that men and women are different and are expected to act differently. Exposure to numerous samples of male and female behavior, dress, and characteristics gradually defines for the child psychosexuality as well as biological sexuality. The differentiated definitions of sex-typed roles then become more and more fixed as his learning and reasoning potential increases. In this view the boy does not identify with or model himself after his father; he more or less models himself after a cognitively derived image of maleness as exemplified by the men in his society and as described by people he meets. He may copy some of his father's qualities, if they meet cultural expectations, and reject other qualities which are not, in the child's view, culturally valued.

Childhood Autism. Psychoses are the most profoundly destructive of personality deviations. They represent the extreme breakdown of psychological and personal functioning. Psychotics are likely to be irrational, suffer from auditory and visual hallucinations, and harbor delusions of grandeur or persecution. They may be almost completely withdrawn. Schizophrenia, one of the most common of the psychoses, occurs in adolescents and adults. In the early years of development, personality disturbances are sometimes observed which seem to be a form of psychosis; they have been labeled childhood schizophrenia by some, and autism or early infantile autism by others. The distinction between childhood schizophrenia and autism is often based upon the age at which the disturbance commences. Children who reveal the symptoms early in life are classified as autistic, whereas those who show characteristic symptoms after a period of fairly normal development are classified as childhood schizophrenics. No matter how they are classified or what diagnostic designation they are assigned, children suffering from this devastating disturbance can readily be distinguished by their behavior and the impact of their illness on their families. Such children may be completely withdrawn, sometimes to the point of mutism. At the other extreme, their behavior may be characterized by violent and bizarre outbursts of running, hitting, and inarticulate screaming. The thought processes of these children do not correspond to those of even the youngest of normal children; thinking is strange, not simply naïve and illogical.

The causes of psychoses in general, and schizophrenia or autism in particular, remain obscure. Theories range from those emphasizing genetic, biological, and chemical influences to others stressing interpersonal and social factors. Treatment may include medication, surgery (more common in the past), and intensive psychotherapy. The prognosis for these children depends in part upon the degree and extensiveness of the disorder. There has been a growing effort on the part of both private and governmental agencies to increase the number of therapeutically oriented schools for autistic and other emotionally disturbed children, and to enlarge the pool of trained personnel to work with these children.

SOCIAL DEVELOPMENT

The child of two is both physically and psychologically ready to become socialized. Whereas an infant's experience with his social environment is circumscribed by lack of mobility and limited communication, the two-year-old is able to move around and explore his surroundings, and make known his needs and desires. He increasingly expresses likes and dislikes in food, clothing, and activities, and he is no longer completely dependent upon his caretakers for company but can play alone and can even enjoy peer companionship for short periods of time.

Just as dependency is the hallmark of infancy, the drive toward autonomy is the major task of the toddler. As he takes initial steps toward self-determination and begins to differentiate between acceptable and nonacceptable behavior, a socialization process is set into motion which continues through childhood and prepares the child to adapt to the mores of his society. First at home, and then later in play groups, the preschool child gradually develops social responsibility and self-control. Through disciplinary practices, role-modeling, and direct teaching, parents and teachers impart to the young the broad social standards of the society as well as immediate codes of conduct which protect the child from harm and lead to harmonious social living.

During toddlerhood, and into the preschool years, the child becomes more and more self-sufficient. By three years of age he can feed himself, using fork and spoon, and almost completely dress himself. Buttons and zippers present a problem until about four years of age, while the complexity of shoe-tying is not overcome until five or six.

Play. Play activity is an important aspect of social development. While infants engage in a form of play, it is solitary in nature and consists mainly of sensorimotor activity, such as waving a hand in the air or babbling. The first sign of social play occurs when the two- or two-and-a-half-year-old begins to enjoy peer companionship. In *parallel play,* one child sits alongside another child; although each child engages in individual pursuits, there is an awareness of sociability. Parallel play progresses to *associative play* when the child accompanies other children in such activities as climbing a monkey-gym or block-building, but still does not actively interact with his playmates. At about three, children participate in *cooperative play*, a relatively organized form of play in which toys are shared and each child makes a contribution to the play situation. Such games as "follow-the-leader" and simple dramatic presentations are examples of cooperative play.

During the preschool years, much of the child's world involves fantasy and *imaginative play*. The preschool child is not yet very self-conscious and he can therefore instantly transform himself into a soaring bird or a television character, without fear of ridicule.

THE FUNCTION OF PLAY. The fact that young children spend most of their waking hours in play needs no explanation. Children are pleasure-oriented, and play is fun. Play, however, has a number of functions beyond that of providing pleasure. As an essentially developmental process, play leads to physical coordination and social facility. Through active play toddlers develop motor coordination which prepares them for participation in the various games of childhood. This in time has an impact on social standing and peer relationships. Children usually admire and choose playmates who are adept in social activities. In the broadest sense, play enables children to try on adult roles and to prepare for a variety of life functions. When little girls and boys play house, when they dress up in parents' clothes, for example, they imitate grown-up roles and situations.

Play also serves as an acceptable vehicle for the release of tension and aggression. While displays of aggressive behavior may not be permissible under usual circumstances, they are tolerated in the competitiveness of play. In the many make-believe games of childhood and in periods of daydreaming, a child is able to try on many different roles and can temporarily overcome some of the inevitable dissatisfactions he is experiencing with the socializing process. It is not unusual for a child to act out the role of a strict father or a demanding mother, thereby assuming a role of power for a brief moment. In this sense, play becomes a safety valve, permitting acceptable release of frustration and negative feelings.

IMAGINARY PLAYMATES. Some children, especially those without siblings or peer companionship, develop imaginary playmates during the preschool years. The imaginary companion may take the form of an animal or another child. This make-believe relationship enables the child to practice social skills and express feelings which might otherwise remain hidden. The verbal by-play with imaginary companions and the situations the child creates with these companions provide the preschool child with a private and safe refuge for companionship of a unique kind. Girls are more inclined to engage in this kind of fantasy than are boys, and the creative and outgoing child is more likely to have an imaginary companion.

Peer Interaction. In most instances children learn socialization skills through association with age-mates; thus the peer group exercises a significant influence on the socialization process. As the preschool child is gently eased out of the home into the playground and nursery school, contacts with peer companions increase. Social interaction, on both group and individual levels, provides an opportunity for practicing and achieving social skills. A study of preschool socialization behavior revealed that children at this age reinforce one another psychologically through expressions of approval and affection, through compliance with each other's demands, and through social rewards. Even negative peer attention was found to provide more social reinforcement than no attention at all (12). As children begin to depend upon their peers for emotional support, adult dependency diminishes.

The Preschool Experience. Whether nursery school attendance contributes to acquisition of socialization skills, and if so, how much, has not been determined conclusively. Some proponents of the preschool experience believe that young children relinquish dependency behavior more readily and make impressive social gains with exposure to a school experience. Others do not consider a structured group activity necessary at this age; a child, they contend, can derive similar benefits from spontaneously formed play groups or casual relationships within the home and neighborhood. Some studies of this subject indicate that the average child usually catches up in the early years of elementary school with the social skills other children have acquired during a preschool experience (23). As indicated earlier, the lasting value of compensatory programs is still a controversial issue. Preschool experiences are usually recommended for children who live in areas that preclude peer companionship and for overly dependent children who need help in disengaging themselves from the home for brief periods of time. Unfortunately, many children are placed in preschool settings of irregular quality for custodial purposes.

It is estimated that more than one-third of the mothers of this country with children under three work outside the home; thus, children very often find themselves in poorly maintained day-care centers and nursery schools for reasons other than social enrichment.

Popularity Determinants. In the early stages of social interaction, choice of playmates is somewhat haphazard, depending largely upon chance opportunity and such prearranged circumstances as parent-organized groups. As children mature during the preschool years, however, their social interactions become more self-determined and systematic. Sociometric testing reveals that five-year-olds, for example, prefer peer companions who have overcome basic dependency needs and do not rely heavily on adults for help. The more popular child, in general, is one who values peer assistance and peer approval, but who is not intrusive. Friendliness, sensitivity, and outgoingness are all attributes which characterize the more sought-after playmate. Several studies find a positive correlation between intelligence and popularity (12). Children of five are decidedly selective in their choice of companions, and preferred relationships persist for extended periods.

Toilet Training. Although toilet training was discussed above in relation to personality development, it merits a special section here as an essential aspect of socialization. One of the major tasks of the preschool child in our society is the establishment of bowel and urinary control. Early toilet-training methods in this country were influenced by the behavioristic philosophy of John S. Watson. During the 1920s and the 1930s parents engaged in rigid habit training in order to achieve control by six or seven months. With the onset of the psychoanalytic and other child-oriented movements, there was a return to the gentler procedures of the pre-Watsonian era. Rather than taking the risk of traumatizing the child by forceful demands, parents became more tolerant and patient. They waited until they saw some evidence of sphincter muscle readiness in their children, usually during the second year of life, before introducing nonthreatening training techniques. Parents from the middle and upper socioeconomic classes today generally use a combination of conditioning and psychoanalytic principles in encouraging their children to cooperate in toilet training. They try to avoid raising fears and anxiety in the child that could lead to later emotional disturbance. Between the middle of the first and second years the mother looks for signals of readiness and then lovingly reinforces appropriate behavior with rewards of food and praise.

In general, bowel control is established early in the second year. Control of urination, however, is a much more erratically timed procedure. Daytime control is usually established first and is achieved by two and a half years of age, whereas nighttime control may not occur until some months later. As a rule, girls become toilet trained earlier than boys.

It is not unusual for a child who has already established good bladder control to have an occasional lapse. Some children wet themselves during the day because they do not want to interrupt play activities to run to the bathroom. Mild emotional disturbances or minor illnesses may also account for infrequent bed-wetting and "accidents." Some children, however, do have persistent bed-wetting problems and may even wet their clothing during the day.

A child should not be considered a chronic bed-wetter or enuretic, however, until he has reached four or five years of age. In many instances the condition is of psychogenic origin, although physical irregularities such as immature bladder or diabetes should first be ruled out. It has been found that some children wet the bed at night because their sleep is so sound that they do not feel the pressure of a full bladder. Some commercial devices which alert the child to bladder tension have been found helpful in this regard.

6

The Middle Years

The years from six to eleven are described as *the middle years of childhood,* or *the school years.* While maintaining close security bonds to his home and family, the child in his middle years explores and consolidates his status in an expanded social peer world. Freud called this stage the *latency period* because he believed it to be a time when the child's emotional and psychological conflicts, particularly his sexual feelings, are quiescent. He is free from the intrusion of adjustment problems observed in earlier years and can now direct his energy toward learning academic skills.

Despite the implication of a quiet and pleasant interlude between early childhood and adolescence inherent in the term "latency," the middle years are a time of internal and external adjustments. Some children make these adjustments with ease; others suffer in varying degrees from exposure to the social and intellectual demands of the period.

The middle years are as fascinating as any other period in the growth cycle. These are years for developing academic skills, fitting into the social world beyond the home, arriving at a workable set of moral standards, and developing a positive psychosexual identification.

PHYSICAL DEVELOPMENT

Bodily functioning and outward appearance are of great concern to the middle-years child. Motor coordination, size, and height take on psychological significance during this growth period because the child's evaluation of himself and of his status depends in such large part on how he literally measures up to his peers. The short girl who cannot reach the pedals of a bicycle and the poorly coordinated boy who cannot throw a ball straight are made keenly aware of their physical inadequacies by more fortunate age-mates who are endowed with sturdier physiques or greater dexterity. The child who cannot keep up with the peer group sometimes suffers social exclusion; the little girl who cannot ride a bike cannot join her friends on neighborhood excursions; and the boy who is not an asset to the team may not be invited to play ball. Sometimes, with improved physical functioning, children overcome these early assaults on the ego, but often the feelings of physical incompetence generated in middle childhood persist into adult life.

Growth patterns are slower in middle childhood than those of the first six years. Toward the close of the period, however, girls begin their preadolescent growth spurt, making noticeable gains in height and weight. Here again, variations in body build can affect psychological equanimity. Early-maturing girls show greater prowess at play, to the consternation of their classmates, especially slow-developing boys. On the other hand, girls who mature more rapidly than their age-mates sometimes see themselves as out of step and feel self-conscious about their appearance.

The period of middle childhood, then, while marked by growth latency, is nevertheless physiologically oriented because success and failure at play and in the classroom (for example, in writing skills, reading, and handcrafts) are so closely related to body performance. Robert Havighurst sees refinement of neuromuscular skills as a primary developmental thrust of the middle years, because such maturation permits the child to enter "the world of games and work." According to Havighurst, the peer group rewards a child for success by according him a position of high esteem and punishes him for failure by indifference or disdain (10).

Growth Rate. The median height for six-year-old girls is about 45.3 inches (115 cm), the median weight about 43 pounds (19 kg). Boys, who from birth have a slight edge over girls in both height and weight, average about an inch taller and about two pounds heavier than girls at the onset of the middle years. This parallel ratio of growth between boys and girls persists until the close of the middle years when girls begin, at about eleven years of age, to overtake boys in size. For the next few years, girls, because of their earlier entrance into puberty, are on the average taller and heavier than boys. In the next chapter, on adolescence, the growth spurt will be discussed in more detail.

It is interesting to compare a schoolyard line-up of first-graders with that of a fifth- or sixth-grade class. In the line of younger children, not only is there very little increase in size between the smallest child at the head of the line and the tallest child at the rear, but also, boys and girls are well interspersed throughout the line. Fifth- and sixth-grade classes, on the other hand, show a much wider variation in size, with the girls likely to be clustered at the tall end of the line.

Body Build. Changes in bodily proportions continue to occur in middle childhood as bone and muscle growth increases. Arms and legs lengthen, and the trunk narrows, giving the child a lanky appearance. The chest broadens, and the child's physique at this midway period between infancy and adolescence more closely resembles the adult frame than that of the potbellied preschooler.

For the most part boys and girls are of equal strength and energy during the middle years and can compete with each other in team games. It is only after boys achieve their growth spurt at about thirteen or fourteen that they begin to surpass girls in muscular ability and endurance. This is not to say that an individual girl may not perform better than her male classmates in tennis or on the baseball field. In general, however, after the onset of adolescence, both women and men prefer to compete against members of their own sex because of the marked differences in physique between the sexes. In some instances girls have insisted that their exclusion from all-boy teams and sports was discriminatory, and the courts have upheld their position.

Sensorimotor Development. Much of a child's success in acquiring such skills as writing, running, and ball-throwing is dependent upon motor coordination. At the start of the elementary school years children have more control over their large muscles than their fine muscles, as evidenced by clumsy and irregular penmanship. By sixth grade, however, small-muscle control has improved considerably. The average eleven-year-old writes, paints, sews, and handles tools with substantial proficiency. Girls tend to excel in fine motor control activities during the years from six to twelve, while boys exhibit greater interest in such gross motor pursuits as throwing and kicking a ball, wrestling, and running. Interest and excellence in these respective areas may be more closely related to cultural preferences between girls and boys than differences in muscular development. With the advent of unisex life styles, girls are participating more and more in activities traditionally considered to be male pursuits, such as Little League baseball, and are consequently developing a higher degree of large-muscle skill than has previously been noted.

Childhood Diseases. In middle childhood the incidence of acute respiratory illness drops sharply. The so-called children's diseases, which usually occur early in middle childhood, are less of a threat to children today because of childhood immunization procedures, increased medical knowledge, and the development of new drugs.

The American Academy of Pediatrics suggests that babies be immunized against diphtheria, tetanus, and whooping cough (DPT shots) at two, four, and six months of age. Oral immunization against polio should also be administered at these ages, and boosters should be given at eighteen months and four and five years of age. Diphtheria-tetanus boosters are due again at fourteen or fifteen, and every ten years thereafter.

To avoid measles and mumps, the child should receive a combined measles-mumps-rubella (German measles) vaccine at twelve months of age. One other precaution prescribed for children is the tuberculin test, which is usually given at twelve months and in adolescence.

Unfortunately parents sometimes neglect to follow through on immunization schedules after the first year of life, and some children contract the aforementioned illnesses during the early school years. Health professionals periodically alert the public to the dangers of inadequate immunization, and most school systems now require verification of immunization upon a child's entrance into elementary school.

MENTAL DEVELOPMENT

Although mental activity is obviously involved in every aspect of the child's daily life, school is the arena where intellectual skills come most clearly into focus. Formal schooling is the central activity of the child's day for many years to come. Thus, mental development in the middle years is expressed most directly by the child's academic accomplishments or failures. In Piaget's terms, the child enters the stage of concrete operations at the beginning of the middle years and progresses to the stage of formal operations at its close. Children from seven to ten reason quite well about concrete phenomena and engage in increasingly more complex cognitive operations and more intricate abstract thinking. By the time they enter adolescence, they are ready to solve problems involving hypotheses and high-level abstractions.

Cognition. Cognitive development, as stated previously, entails maturation and experience. As biological and neurological structures mature, the child becomes better able to realize and express his intellectual potential.

With experience, the child learns to use such units as symbols, concepts, and rules. He expands his egocentric and simplistic view of phenomena and has a better understanding of causality. In the early stages of childhood, children think in animistic terms. They account for causality by attributing lifelike characteristics to inanimate objects; a clock is considered to be alive because it ticks and its hands move. Similarly, they invoke magical thinking to explain the unfathomable. Thus, a young child will attribute powers of omniscience to a parent who discovers that the child took a cookie, although the parent did not observe the act.

Not until children are well into the middle years are they able to handle abstract concepts effectively, engage in higher-level objectification, and make varied and complex classifications. Thinking becomes more logical and realistic, and the child begins to achieve a more valid understanding of abstract phenomena such as causality. As logical thinking increases, animistic and magical thinking diminish.

Experience and skill in the use of symbols and concepts are prerequisites to learning a language and learning to read. The preschool child may dabble with word sounds, but the child of the middle years plays with words in terms of symbols and meanings. He is intrigued by word games in which the letters are scrambled. Such peer group rituals as developing passwords and coded messages are taken very seriously. As his use of symbols and other cognitive units becomes more refined, the child learns to read books and magazines and his knowledge increases. His ability to recognize similarities, to be more objective, and to conceptualize the future all represent a considerable advance in cognitive development.

Issues arising from the meaning and significance of intelligence and cognition in our culture have stimulated the development of many theories and controversies. Among current theories concerned with cognition are learning theory, information-processing theory, and structural theory. There are points of agreement as well as disagreement among theorists. McCandless and Trotter state: "The most important difference among the theories has to do with the age at which children are able to solve certain problems. Learning theory and information-processing theory suggest that any subject can be taught to any child if that child has had the necessary background or experience and if the subject is presented in the appropriate form. . . . Structural theory, on the other hand, suggests that some things just cannot be understood until a child's mind has reached a certain stage of biological development, no matter how much experience or training the child receives" (21, p. 280). All of these theories, however, stress the importance of environmental stimulation.

LEARNING THEORY. According to learning theory, cognition results from the impact on the child of experiences and observations, followed by association and reinforcement (13). The child responds to varying situations and repeats his response until he has built up numerous behavioral patterns which can be generalized and transferred to other situations. In this way, according to the learning theorists, the child increases the scope and complexity of his thinking processes.

INFORMATION-PROCESSING THEORY: BRUNER'S STAGES OF COGNITIVE DEVELOPMENT (4). Cognitive development and cognition have been compared to computer programing. Information is received and processed by the child through experience. The child does not simply learn the units that constitute informational input; he also develops rules for programing and processing that information. The older child with more experience will employ more numerous and more complex rules for processing and solving problems.

Jerome Bruner has been classified by some as an information-processing theorist because of his concern with the process by which a child's experiences are encoded and stored. He has also been placed among the maturational and stage theorists because he has identified various stages of cognitive development. Bruner's stages, which he calls modes of representations and which relate to how experiences are taken in and interpreted by the child, are as follows:

The Enactive Representation of Early Infancy. At this stage, the child encodes and stores the objects and experiences he encounters in terms of the behavioral meaning they have for him, the actions they elicit from him. A nipple evokes a lip-pursing response. The nipple is encoded and stored by this physical enactment.

The Ikonic Representation of Later Infancy and Toddlerhood. This is the period in which the objects the child encounters and the events he experiences are viewed and encoded as images or visual representations. This representational skill enlarges the child's cognitive repertoire, and he can now "think" in terms of absent objects or past events.

The Symbolic Representation of the Preschooler. In this period the child begins to use language as an essential vehicle in cognition. He is able to represent objects and events abstractly and symbolically, rather than in the concrete form of the actual object or its image. This stage evolves over a long period of time, becoming well established in the middle years. The ability to use symbolic representation increases the child's understanding and effectiveness in managing the events and problems of his life.

Bruner does not view his stages as successive; rather, he sees them as representational modes which are operative concurrently once they have developed. Bruner also believes that learning need not be related to maturation and that it can be accelerated by proper teaching. He says: "Any idea or problem or body of knowledge can be presented in a form simple enough so that any particular learner can understand it in a recognizable form" (4, p. 44). Bruner calls the idea of maturational readiness a "mischievous half-truth" and believes that readiness is taught; "one does not simply wait for it."

STRUCTURAL THEORY: PIAGET'S STAGE OF CONCRETE OPERATIONS. Piaget's scheme of cognitive development is the most clearly and elaborately developed system of structural theory. He differs from Bruner in his belief that cognitive development follows a sequential pattern and that children learn only what they are maturationally ready to learn, although environmental facilitation may be helpful. When children reach school age they become more flexible in their thinking and engage in mental operations at a less egocentric level. Nevertheless, their ability to generalize and abstract is still limited, hence the name of the stage, *concrete operations.* Children in this stage understand best what they can see and feel. Symbolic thinking does increase during this period, however, and children begin to develop systematic approaches toward understanding physical phenomena and solving problems. They are expanding their cognitive skills in preparation for the more advanced forms of thinking required in academic learning.

DECENTRATION AND CLASS INCLUSION. During the period of concrete operations children develop an awareness of groupings and begin to classify objects in logical order. They can sort objects by size, color, and quantity simultaneously, rather than focusing on one characteristic only. This ability enables the child to understand that any single object in a group may be included in a number of different subgroupings, depending on the way in which objects are classified.

CONSERVATION. Another characteristic of this period is the growing ability of the child to understand the principle of conservation. He begins to see that certain quantitative properties of objects remain constant despite external changes (length, amount, and volume). The quantity of a substance, such as a lump of clay, remains the same whether it is made into a ball or shaped like a cigar. Similarly, the amount of water in a container remains constant whether it is poured into a low squat beaker or into a tall tubular vase.

REVERSIBILITY. The ability to understand the principles of classification and conservation is closely related to the comprehension of reversibility. Round red disks culled out of a group of disks can be mixed into the group again, and a clay ball that has been changed into a cigar can be restored to its original form. When the child comprehends that a process can be reversed, he can apply this concept to relative locations of objects (up or down) and to personal relationships (the fact that a boy has a sister means that a sister has a brother); each has a reversible counterpart, down to up and sister to brother.

SERIATION. A further essential cognitive skill which develops during this period is the ability to order objects sequentially and systematically. Thus, children are able to see the logic of sorting objects according to size (smallest to largest). This skill increases awareness of relationships and becomes a major function in learning arithmetical concepts.

Intelligence. Perhaps the most significant and controversial aspect of cognitive development is the study of intelligence: its definition, its nature, and its measurement. Just as individual children differ from one another in size, shape, weight, facial expressions, physical abilities, and voice intonations, they differ too in the degree to which they remember, in what they remember, and in their ability to learn cognitive skills and to perform such cognitive tasks as reading and arithmetic. These individual differences and their implications underlie many of the controversies surrounding the study of intelligence.

DEFINITION. Definitions of intelligence usually include the verbal and academic functions of cognition: memory, abstractive ability, reasoning, ability to generalize and solve problems, and the capacity to adapt old learning to new situations. Some authorities believe that a true definition of intelligence should include nonverbal skills (music, art, dance, and mechanical ability) and social skills (the "street-wise child") as well. In any event, children vary in their ability to acquire such skills. Why such differences occur, what they mean, and how they can be reduced are questions that are pragmatically and theoretically crucial. These considerations have, however, been confused at times by emotionalized intrusions. Intelligence is not a neutral word in Western culture; it carries many value connotations. Intelligence is often equated with better or worse, desirable or undesirable. Most people, of course, object to being categorized as part of a group that is considered inferior, or even average or ordinary. Thus, if the definition can be changed, the composition of the groupings may then be changed, with a consequent reassignment of one's place among the groups.

David Wechsler, who developed one of the most widely used individual intelligence tests, defines intelligence as "the aggregate or global capacity of the individual to act purposively, to think rationally, and to deal effectively with his environment" (29, p. 3). In the 1974 revision of his test, Wechsler modified the definition somewhat by stating: "Intelligence is the overall capacity of the individual to understand and cope with the world around him" (30, p. 7).

In the manual for the 1960 revision of the Stanford-Binet Intelligence Scale (27), another widely used individual intelligence test, the authors explain the basis for their test in terms that, in effect, define intelligence as the ability to solve problems. Among the cognitive skills they consider prerequisite for problem solving are retention and retrieval of information (memory), the ability to abstract and generalize, the ability to reason and understand, and the ability to apply these skills toward solving problems and adapting to life situations.

All of the definitions set forth above are subject to interpretation. Can a definition of intelligence encompass the abilities of children of diverse cultural backgrounds and cognitive interest and styles? Does the expression of cognitive skill in verbal areas, which is the core of most school curriculums, take precedence over the manipulation of cognitive skills in less verbal and less academic ways? Should the child who does extremely well in school be considered more intelligent than the one who does poorly in school but who is highly adaptable? The "street-wise" child certainly is solving problems and adapting to his environment. He may, however, be unable to read or solve mathematical problems at grade level.

What, then, is the nature of intelligence? Intelligence is seen by some as a synthesis of various cognitive skills, thereby recognizing that different kinds of functioning enter into intelligence. "Intelligent" behavior is thus conceived as a melding of separate components. Individuals do not fragment their abilities to abstract, to develop vocabularies, to reason, or to remember; all of these cognitive activities work together simultaneously as part of overall functioning. The common element in these skills, the characteristic known as intelligence, has been called the general or "g" factor. The Stanford-Binet Intelligence Scale is based on the "g" factor.

At the other extreme are theorists who believe that intelligence is composed of clearly differentiated, specific, or "s" factors. L. L. Thurstone, for example, has developed a test based on seven primary or specific abilities (28). J. P. Guilford has gone further in this direction and has proposed a "structure of intellect" composed of 120 factors (9). The multifactor approach attempts to collect these many similarities and differences in functioning under the comprehensive term "intelligence."

INTELLIGENCE TESTING. Although it is difficult to define and explain intelligence, the measurement of this elusive quality is commonly undertaken, directly and indirectly, subjectively and objectively. We subconsciously judge the intelligence of friends when they discuss current issues. We evaluate their intellectual ability by their occupation, income, education, and social status. Children are formally tested and graded in school, and their progress or lack of achievement is frequently ascribed to intellectual capacity.

Since the development of the Binet-Simon tests in 1905, many other individual and group tests have been devised to measure intelligence. The Binet-Simon tests were originally designed to help teachers in French schools identify mentally retarded children. The tests became so useful and popular that a number of American psychologists, including Goddard, Kuhlman, and Terman, adapted them for use in the United States.

THE STANFORD-BINET INTELLIGENCE SCALE. The so-called Stanford revision of the Binet tests was first published by Lewis Terman and his colleagues at Stanford University in 1916. In his revision Terman used the Intelligence Quotient (IQ), introduced by the German psychologist William Stern, as a measure of intelligence to provide a score that would have the same meaning across all ages (26).

The Stanford-Binet Scales have been revised and standardized several times since 1916. Standardization is a procedure used to ensure the adequacy and appropriateness of a test item in relation to the population being surveyed. Tests are standardized by administering them to a representative cross section of the population before they are put into general use. Many intelligence tests, particularly those used in the past, have been standardized on samples that excluded such major segments of the population as the rural poor and black children. Although the revisers of the Stanford-Binet in 1937 set out to obtain a standardization in terms of age, sex, geography, and socioeconomic status, it now appears that persons from urban areas with higher than average socioeconomic backgrounds were overrepresented. Furthermore, the standardization sample included only native-born white individuals. Although the validity of the test items was not tried out on blacks, Indians, and Mexican-Americans, this test was and continues to be used to evaluate the intelligence of children from those groups.

The Stanford-Binet is individually administered. Although it provides scores for children from two years of age through adulthood, it generally is not given after elementary school age. The Binet, as it is commonly known, consists of questions and tasks grouped into progressively higher age levels. Each test item is given a one- or two-month value so that a child passing all six items at the seven-year level is given twelve months of credit; if he passes five of the six items, he receives ten months' credit. The testing terminates when the child reaches an age level at which all items are failed. The test score is obtained by totaling all the months for which the child has been given credit, and is expressed in terms of mental age. In effect, the child is being compared with other children of similar and different ages. Thus, a seven-year-old who passes all test items through the seven-year level is credited with 84 months, or a mental age of seven. He is therefore intellectually on a par with other seven-year-olds. If he were credited with only 72 months, he would have a mental age of six and would more closely reflect the intellectual development of a six-year-old. He would then be considered intellectually slower than average.

The *intelligence quotient* or IQ refers to a score that reflects in a single number the child's deviation from his chronological age. The score is computed by dividing the mental age by the chronological age and multiplying by 100. An IQ of 100 represents the score expected of a child who is functioning intellectually at his chronological age level. An IQ score of above or below 100 indicates the degree of deviation. A seven-year-old who obtains an IQ of 86 would have a mental age of 6:

$$IQ = \frac{MA\ (6)}{CA\ (7)} \times 100$$

The Stanford-Binet is essentially a verbal test; however, some of the questions require the child to manipulate such objects as wooden cubes and beads. It includes a vocabulary definition test (replaced at younger levels by picture recognition), definition and use of abstract words, recognition of situational absurdities, and recall of numbers, sentences, and object configuration.

The Binet has been widely used as a predictor of academic achievement. Inasmuch as the test is primarily verbal in nature and many of its questions test skills that are taught in school, this instrument has shown a high correlation with school achievement.

THE WECHSLER INTELLIGENCE SCALES. The intelligence scales devised by David Wechsler test individuals ranging in age from four years to adulthood:

The Wechsler Preschool and Primary Scale of Intelligence (WPPSI): ages 4 to 6½.

The Wechsler Intelligence Scale for Children—Revised (WISC-R): ages 6 to 16 (actually 16 years 11 months and 30 days).

The Wechsler Adult Intelligence Scale (WAIS): ages 16 and older.

Like the Stanford-Binet, the Wechsler scales are individually administered.

The Wechsler scales differ from the Stanford-Binet test in the following ways:

1. Test items in the Wechsler scales are arranged according to abilities, skills, or knowledge rather than according to age level. Therefore, the Wechsler scales include such brief subtest batteries as information, comprehension, arithmetic, block design, picture arrangement, and picture completion. Each subtest is scored separately and computed into an overall score based on all subtest results.

2. Test items are separated into verbal and performance batteries. For example, vocabulary, similarities, and comprehension are included in the verbal batteries; block design, picture arrangement, and object assembly are subtests in the performance batteries.

3. The Wechsler scales do not use mental age as the basis for computing the IQ; it is statistically computed. Points are assigned to each successfully completed item. (In the performance items, time and speed are scorable factors.) The results are then translated into weighted or scaled scores, which are totaled for each of the two batteries. These scores, added together, give the full-scale score. The verbal IQ, the performance IQ, and the full-scale IQ are obtained by consulting the standardized age-graded tables provided with the kit.

4. In revealing differential levels of ability on different types of subtests of related skills, the Wechsler scales provide data that may be used for diagnostic purposes beyond the simple measurement of intelligence.

The Wechsler verbal IQ shows positive correlations with the Stanford-Binet and with other tests that lean heavily on verbal skills. Like the Binet, the Wechsler also reflects school achievement. The performance IQ correlates best with tests of nonverbal ability. Correlations are generally higher between verbal tests and the verbal IQ of the Wechsler than between these tests and the full-scale IQ. Nevertheless, the correlations are high enough to indicate that the full-scale score of the Wechsler is similar to the estimate of intelligence provided by these tests. The Wechsler is criticized and praised for the same shortcomings and strengths ascribed to any of the tests to which it is compared.

GROUP TESTS. These are paper-and-pencil tests with time limits, administered to a group of children. Test instructions are presented to the child either orally or in writing in a test booklet. Test items are similar to those in individually administered tests. Although most group tests require reading and writing skills, particularly at the upper levels, some are nonverbal.

Group intelligence tests are economical because they can be administered to many children at a time, but unfortunately, they are open to many intrusions which may invalidate the results. Time limits may not be diligently observed, for example, or a child may daydream and allow his attention to wander so that he does not complete as many items as he might if the test were administered individually. The child's language and reading ability may not be on a level with his intellectual ability, which will affect his scores adversely on a group intelligence test. However, when administered properly, group tests provide rough indices of intellectual ability.

A CRITIQUE OF INTELLIGENCE TESTING. The evaluation of any intelligence test must take into account the assumptions on which it is based and the uses to which it is put. Intelligence cannot be directly seen or measured; it must be inferred from the child's responses to specific tasks. For example, when a child is asked how an apple and a banana are alike, his response gives clues to his degree of intelligence. He must be able to recall the nature of both apple and banana, to differentiate and generalize, and to articulate the similarities.

Intelligence tests have been criticized for inferring intelligence on the basis of a child's responses to tasks that are heavily weighted in favor of verbal cognitive skills and abilities that are valued and nurtured in middle- or upper-class homes. These tests, the critics say, do not measure skills that are encouraged in children from lower-income families or minority groups. Such instruments should be discarded, it is asserted, because they discriminate, are culturally biased, and unfairly stigmatize minority children. Since intelligence test scores influence school and class placement, college admissions, and career-guidance practices, minority children are regularly and perhaps unfairly directed into less intellectually demanding and less rewarding school programs and careers.

Advocates of intelligence testing agree that these tests are weighted in favor of verbal skills and that they do indeed measure the degree to which a child has absorbed knowledge, in and out of school. They do not believe, however, that these characteristics of intelligence tests invalidate them. Proponents of testing argue that the majority culture determines the intellectual skills which lead to success in a society. Standard English is the language of the majority and must be the verbal medium through which children are taught and evaluated in the schools. The tests, they say, discriminate between children on the basis of their ability to grasp complex ideas and solve intellectually based problems. From the pool of children who can solve problems accurately and quickly and perform complex mental operations will come the scientists, researchers, philosophers, and other creative thinkers of the future. Intelligence tests have been able to identify many of these children. Musical, artistic, athletic, and social skills, the test defenders say, have great value to the individual and to society, but are not singled out in intelligence testing. Boxers, football players, and rock musicians, while paid very high salaries, do not have skills which of themselves indicate high intelligence. This discrepancy is not the fault of the test, they say, but rather the result of the values and priorities society has established. In response to the argument that tests penalize children for their non-normative cultural and ethnic background, the advocates of intelligence testing assert that the blame must be assigned not to the test but to the individuals who misuse it. Tests should be used as but one of many tools to help teach and guide children, and should not be treated as infallible indicators of future achievement. Such other factors as motivation, emotional stability, socioeconomic disadvantages, and family aspirations should be considered along with test results in making evaluations.

Attempts have been made to devise culture-free tests which would equalize the individual differences that are said to make the regularly used tests invalid. Most of these culture-free tests are nonverbal and pictorial in form, although instructions may be written or oral. To isolate cultural and environmental components from tests is, however, difficult. Children learn to interpret and understand the symbols that surround them in the culture in which they are reared, and a test question must contain familiar material. Culture-free tests should include items with which children from all strata of society, and all cultural and ethnic groups, are familiar, a goal which has proved difficult to achieve. Those culture-free tests which have been developed are not used widely because their value has not as yet been established.

The IQ, the intelligence quotient, is one of the most controversial measures in psychology. Far from being precise, as it is frequently considered to be, an IQ score may have a random error of plus or minus five points. In general, IQ scores become more stable as the child grows older; IQs obtained when a child is two years of age will show less difference from the same child's IQ at five years of age than it will from his IQ at age nine. Less variation will be revealed between nine and twelve and even less between twelve and twenty, but there are indeed individual children who show marked changes in IQ score from one age to another.

Because the IQ is dependent on many factors, a crucial change in the child's life may be reflected in his IQ. For example, an unhappy or depressed child who has been abandoned by his parents may show an increase in IQ when he is adopted and becomes part of a secure happy family. Changes in socioeconomic status, physical condition, peer group affiliation and motivation, or any other number of other conditions may lead to minor or marked changes in IQ. As previously stated, intelligence is a function of both heredity and environment; it is not the exclusive province of either. The IQ, however, because it is a measure, is particularly responsive to environmental factors such as cultural attitudes toward learning, anxiety factors, and availability of sources of information, including books and magazines. It is also affected by nonintellectual influences such as physically based disabilities (e.g., dyslexia).

Moral Development. An important aspect of the child's development is the ability to make moral judgments and to adhere to moral standards acceptable to himself and to society. Although it begins at an earlier stage and is not completed until adulthood, moral development is one of the crucial developmental tasks of the middle years.

PIAGET'S STAGES OF MORAL DEVELOPMENT (25). Piagetian theory relates moral development to intellectual growth. The cognitive skills required to make judgments parallel Piaget's stages of mental development. The preoperational child is egocentric and is unable to decenter (to focus on or consider more than one characteristic of an object or situation at a time) in his daily life. Therefore preschool children and younger middle-years children are in a stage of *moral realism* because they cannot adjust to mitigating circumstances or see a situation in its context. Each "right" or "just" behavior set down for a particular situation is the only "right" or "just" behavior; no leeway or allowance is permitted. Thus, if a preschooler inadvertently breaks a glass, his playmates are likely to consider this to be as punishable an offense as if the glass were smashed deliberately. Also, they would judge the accidental breaking of many glasses as more deserving of punishment than the deliberate breaking of one glass.

As the child progresses from the preoperational stage through the stage of concrete operations, which covers most of the middle-years period, he becomes less egocentric and more socialized, and able to decenter. He then begins to be capable of *moral relativism,* which is not fully achieved until the stage of formal operations in adolescence. By the end of the middle years he has become more flexible in his thinking and can make moral judgments based on reasoning rather than on absolute standards.

KOHLBERG'S STAGES OF MORAL DEVELOPMENT (18). Lawrence Kohlberg has proposed three main cognitive-developmental levels of moral development which he further divides into six successive stages. Like Piaget, Kohlberg believes in sequential levels of understanding. At each stage, however, a particular child reveals remnants of a previous level of moral thinking and at the same time shows signs of the thinking characteristics of a later stage. The three levels and inclusive stages are as follows:

Level I. Preconventional or Premoral Level. The child views situations in concrete terms of personal and physical reward or punishment.

Stage 1. Obedience and punishment orientation. The child does what is demanded of him to avoid punishment. Right and wrong are determined by punishment meted out and by the approval or disapproval of the accepted authority (usually the mother or father).

Stage 2. Naïve hedonism. Moral thinking is geared toward pleasure seeking. The rightness or wrongness of an act is determined by the degree of benefit derived, primarily by the child, although the needs of others may be considered in the sense of "you do for me and I'll do for you."

Level II. Conventional Level. When the child reaches this level, the wishes and needs of the group (family, peer group, nation) are considered the bases for determining right and wrong.

Stage 3: Maintaining good relations. Rightness means conformity, loyalty, and obtaining approval from the group; it has been called the "good boy–nice girl" stage.

Stage 4: The law-and-order period. The child accepts the rules and laws set down by the family and by his society, more out of respect for authority than fear of punishment.

Level III. Post-Conventional Level. At this point in his development the child makes moral judgments according to abstract principles which can transcend specific group rules and personal needs.

Stage 5: Morality of contract and individual rights. The young person is aware of abstract social morality as defined by the broader social group. Constitutionally protected rights, personal needs relative to the needs of others, and the acceptance of flexibility of interpretation and the changeability of law are fundamental in the determination of right and wrong.

Stage 6: Morality of individual principles of conscience. Moral judgment stems from ethical principles and truths that may transcend the law. Human dignity and respect for human life as a universal principle are crucial considerations.

Although Kohlberg sees the child passing sequentially through these stages, he allows that many do not develop moral judgments beyond the second level, which is that attained in the middle years.

Both Piaget and Kohlberg find moral development intimately related to cognitive growth. Other writers place more emphasis on the influence of emotional and nonintellectual spheres of personality. Psychoanalytic theorists, for example, see the sense of right and wrong evolving from the identification process. As the child struggles with the problems posed by the psychosexual stages and as he resolves his Oedipal conflict, he establishes a deeper identification with his parents. He internalizes their prohibitions (do's and don'ts) so that they become his. The child thus acquires a body of moral values that forms the basis of his conscience or superego.

Although moral development is gauged through the moral judgments a child articulates, the child's behavior in related situations does not always correspond. He may know right from wrong and verbalize higher levels of moral development but act contrary to his knowledge. These findings indicate that moral development should be seen as part of the total personality rather than as a function of cognitive growth alone.

PERSONALITY DEVELOPMENT

Although the personality of the middle-years child may be relatively stable and free from the sexual and emotional pressures of earlier years, many physical, mental, and social changes are taking place which affect personality development.

Freud's Latency Period. According to Freud, psychological conflicts centering on oral, anal, and phallic gratification are major developmental issues for the child from infancy through the preschool years. These concerns culminate in the resolution of the Oedipal conflict. The child then enters latency, a period of psychological calm in which concerns rooted in sexuality lie dormant, along with an unresolved residue from the conflicts experienced in infancy, toddlerhood, and the preschool years. Latency comes to a rather abrupt end in adolescence. The relative quiescence of this period, according to Freudian theory, frees the child to think more objectively, to learn, and to reason. Thus the middle years are core years for school learning.

Although the period from six to eleven is school-oriented in Western society, the issue whether the child at this time is unconcerned with sex and sexuality is open to question. Middle-years children tend to associate with same-sex peers. They are clearly aware of sex differences, are titillated by sexual innuendoes in words, situations, and pictures, and frequently engage in scatological language. Thus Freud's designation of the period as one of sexual latency may be misleading. Nevertheless, the emotional component, or at least the display of intense emotionality surrounding sexuality, does seem to be reduced if not dormant during this period. The sexual questions and off-color bantering appear to be intellectualized rather than emotionalized. Freud's views on latency may indeed be valid insofar as the intellect is dominant over emotions as the child in the middle years explores his sexual self.

Sex Roles. As we have seen, psychosexual identification is one of the major developmental tasks of the preschool years. Havighurst lists the need to develop an appropriate sex role as one of the significant tasks of this period. How children define themselves in terms of femaleness or maleness is an essential ingredient of their self-concept. In the middle years, the distinction between the sexes is taken more seriously, for now it is seen primarily in terms of appropriate role behavior. The child of six or seven is no longer considered to be a "baby" and therefore is encouraged and pressured to conform to the sex-role behavior of the adult. He is not to walk freely about the house undressed. He is not to enter a lavatory or fitting room for the opposite sex. He is not to indulge in overt sexual behavior. His sex-role-associated behavior is also under careful scrutiny. A six- or seven-year-old boy arouses concern in his parents when he is found playing with dolls. Boys who indulge in feminine-type activities raise more anxiety in adults than do girls who prefer the more rough-and-tumble behavior of boys.

The school, along with parents, defines and reinforces appropriate sex-typed behavior in accordance with societal expectations. Although nursery school may have had coed toilets, elementary school lavatories are clearly segregated according to sex. Whether deliberately or not, many playground activities are divided so that girls skip rope and play hopscotch while boys play football or basketball. Only recently have girls been granted membership on teams formerly restricted to boys. By the time children are eight, if not earlier, the social indoctrination surrounding sex-typing has taken a firm internalized hold. It is quite common for boys of this age to gravitate to guns and swords in the playroom, while girls turn to the blackboard or cluster around dolls. By adolescence, the definition of sex role is clear.

Family Influences on Personality Development. Parents and siblings have important effects on personality development.

PARENTAL INFLUENCES. Parents continue to exert a major influence on the child's developing personality throughout the middle years. In many ways parents' own personalities define the nature of their influence. Child-rearing methods are expressions of the attitudes and feelings parents have toward children, parenthood, and discipline. Middle childhood brings a relaxation of some parental pressures and an intensification of others. There is less need for constant supervision and admonition, for example, because the child is in school most of the day. Thus, both parent and child are relieved of the usual tensions arising from constant proximity. Toilet training has been completed, adequate eating and dressing habits have been established, and it is no longer necessary for parents to seek out peer companionship for their children. However, as the child becomes more mobile and is exposed to unfamiliar customs, languages, and loyalties, the concerns of parents shift, and their personality-derived pressures on the child take new forms. Earlier concerns about basic functioning such as toilet training give way to prohibition regarding choice of friends and language.

The loosening of family ties as the child reaches the middle years evokes positive, negative, or mixed reactions on the part of parents. Conscious and unconscious feelings about their children and their own role may lead parents to react ambivalently toward their growing children. For example, a parent might subtly discourage the child from forming the multiple loyalties necessary for growth and adjustment. Or, a parent might use the child's increased mobility and independence as a means of expressing rejection. A child might be sent to friends for the weekend, enrolled in extracurricular activities, or left to his own devices after school. The effect on the child depends on the deep, usually unconscious motivation of the parents and on the appropriateness of the activities thrust upon him.

An extensively investigated area of parental influence on personality development is the kind of discipline or control exerted in the home (2). Is the home authoritarian or overly permissive? Is control exerted arbitrarily with no opportunity for the child to participate in decisions, or is it handled democratically? Homes characterized by consistency, appropriate firmness without arbitrariness, and affection for and acceptance of the child (though not necessarily of his behavior) have been found to be most conducive to the development of mentally healthy, self-sufficient, and well-adjusted children. Children growing up in overly permissive or lax homes, or in overly restrictive, authoritarian family settings find it difficult to develop the self-determination and self-confidence necessary to define the expectations and limits of acceptable social behavior. The permissive parent does not provide the child with sufficient guidance or structure; the restrictive parent inhibits development of the sense of autonomy that comes from exploring, trying out, and questioning in an atmosphere of protected warmth.

SIBLING INFLUENCES. The child's brothers and sisters are an integral part of his daily life from the moment of birth. They contribute in large measure to the family environment and thus affect him directly and indirectly, positively and negatively. The phenomenon of sibling rivalry is well known. In a family of six children interviewed by one of the authors, each child expressed the feeling that he was least favored by his parents. The jealousy evidenced by this comment may cause psychological and behavioral conflict. Studies of sibling influence have shown that birth order, sex of siblings, and age differences have an impact on personality development (1, 17). The oldest child in the family, for example, has been found to be more socially conforming, more conscientious, more responsible, and more likely to adhere to parental wishes and values than later-born children. There is also evidence that children with male siblings are more likely to develop such masculine-typed personality characteristics as aggressiveness, competitiveness, and a tendency to daring than are children without brothers. Another finding correlates extent of rivalry between siblings with age differences. Siblings two to four years apart in age seem to have more problems in relating to each other than do siblings with either less than two or more than four years between them. Other factors that influence sibling relationships are the particular qualities of the sibling, the degree of emotional stability of the child, the physical characteristics of the child and sibling, and parental attitudes toward each child in the family.

Personality Testing. As scientists differentiate and work with segments of human functioning, they employ a variety of measuring techniques. Tests have been developed to measure intelligence, aptitudes, achievement, vision, hearing, and motor skills. Personality has not escaped the scrutiny of measuring and evaluating devices.

Personality tests are designed to elicit characteristic modes of response which may then provide insights into the child's personality traits. These tests measure feelings of affection, hostility, assertiveness, defeat, and ambition, and the extent to which these feelings affect behavior. They are sometimes used to evaluate degree of adjustment or maladjustment and the causes for various symptoms present in the child.

There are three types of personality tests: paper-and-pencil tests, observation tests, and projective techniques. With the exception of paper-and-pencil and questionnaire-type tests, most instruments used in personality evaluation make the assumption that the child's response to a test situation represents a sample of his behavior, which in turn is a product of the combined forces of his personality. As these responses are interpreted, a view of the child's underlying personality emerges.

PAPER-AND-PENCIL TESTS. These tests generally consist of multiple-choice questions. Resulting scores provide a measure of various personality dimensions. One widely used test in this category is the Minnesota Multiphasic Personality Inventory (MMPI). It consists of some 550 statements (there are abbreviated forms) covering such subjects as attitudes toward family, recollections of events, physical health, and others. The MMPI is not used with children of this age, but a simplified version, the Children's Manifest Anxiety Scale (CMAS), is available.

OBSERVATION TESTS. Here the child is observed in special situations, as with other children, in a playroom, or in an interview. Inferences are drawn from these observations relating to the child's personality characteristics.

PROJECTIVE TECHNIQUES. In this type of testing the child is presented with ambiguous situations, tasks, or pictures which presumably elicit characteristic modes of personality reactions. Among this type of test are the Rorschach inkblot test, in which the child is asked to respond to a series of inkblot impressions; the Thematic Apperception Test (TAT), or other picture-story tests, in which the child is asked to make up stories relating to a set of pictures; the Figure Drawing Test, in which the child is asked to draw a person (or a family, or himself); the HTP test (for house, tree, person), in which the child is asked to draw a house, a tree, and a person; and the Bender-Gestalt Visual Motor Test, which requires the child to copy a set of designs.

Projective tests are extremely subjective, and must therefore be interpreted by experienced psychologists.

SOCIAL DEVELOPMENT

The middle years present great challenges in terms of social development. Many children must, for the first time, relinquish the security of the home for a more impersonalized and formal setting. Although it is true that the preschooler ventures out for a few hours at a time to attend a play group or nursery school, he touches home base frequently and relates essentially to one caretaker. With the advent of the formal school years, the child must leave the home for longer hours and relate not only to his classmates but also to a variety of adults such as bus drivers, teachers, and various school personnel.

The school soon becomes the central force in the child's life. Peers and teachers become important socializing agents who, while not supplanting parental models, provide the child with additional standards of socialization.

The early school years impose heavy demands on the child's ability to adjust, requiring a continual process of adaptation within a comparatively short period of time. A six- or seven-year-old must acclimate himself to new surroundings and find acceptance and belonging in a new group, with new surrogates, new rules, and new demands. Some school systems incorporate special group-learning experiences into the curriculum which foster feelings of well-being and provide emotional support during this critical growth period. In such programs children share their concerns and, in so doing, gain strength from each other.

While the middle years evoke feelings of vulnerability, they are also years of pure joy. No longer under the parental thumb, the elementary school child is free to roam farther from home and become part of a subculture of his peers. Many of the happy memories of childhood are associated with this period of life when children enter a secret world of their own, with their own rules and their own language. Unlike the peer society of adolescence, the peer groups of childhood are not in conflict with the adult world. These children are still sufficiently in tune with parents to permit harmonious coexistence. In fact, the child of this period is constantly taking refuge from the many frustrations he faces during the course of the day, and he freely seeks out parental reassurance and support.

In considering the various aspects of social development we must bear in mind that we do not live in a homogeneous society. All children do not share the same experiences and therefore do not have similar patterns of social development. Margaret Mead, in her studies of primitive societies, emphasized the concept of "cultural relativity" (a term attributed to Ruth Benedict) by describing the disparities in behavior that existed among the three New Guinea tribes she observed (22). In contemporary American society there are similar examples of the impact of cultural differences on behavior. For example, children from lower socioeconomic backgrounds begin the separation from home much earlier than six years of age. As infants they may have been brought to a neighborhood sitter, and later, in the toddler period and preschool years, they may have spent the entire day at a child-care center.

Although there are some games that all children have played for many hundreds of years (tag, marbles, jacks), children growing up in rural areas play different games and have different interests and hobbies than city-born children. Peer group activities of the country child may revolve around raising animals (4-H Clubs), whereas the inner-city child may be primarily involved in street-gang behavior. In each instance the peer culture is influenced to a large extent by environmental circumstances, and therefore only the broadest of generalizations can be made regarding the course of social development as it pertains to this age.

Sex Cleavage. During the middle years, girls and boys prefer to socialize with members of their own sex. Between the ages of eight and ten, the sexes go their separate ways—at least in public.

The traditional explanation for this separation of the sexes assumes that boys and girls have different interests. Girls are said to prefer such sex-typed activities as playing house and school, while boys like contact sports and mechanical activities such as building a radio. Consistent with the present-day trend toward enhancing the female role and overcoming sexual stereotypes, some girls are crossing over the line and entering into male athletics and other male-typed pursuits. While this is not as yet a predominant pattern of behavior in middle childhood, the sexual polarization characteristic of this age may be expected to lessen considerably as time goes on.

Toward the end of middle childhood, during the so-called preadolescent years, many incursions are made by both sexes into opposite-sex strongholds, in anticipation of the heterosexual relationships of adolescence. At first, such intrusions are met with exaggerated hostility, but a gradual camaraderie develops which heralds the removal of the barriers between the sexes.

Peer Culture. Despite the divergence of the sexes during middle childhood, the leisure-time interests of boys and girls at this age are fairly similar. Both sexes enjoy biking, swimming, skating, watching television, reading, collecting things (stamps, dolls, comic books, gum wrappers), and playing a variety of sedentary and active games.

During the early portion of the middle-years continuum, boys and girls belong to informally organized play groups that have few rules and little specificity of agenda. Two or three girls who are "best friends" may get together after school just to sit on a stoop and talk or play with their dolls. Several boys may meet at one or another's homes to construct model cars, then wind up the afternoon by raiding a nearby girls' group. As children move further into this period, groups become more formal and secretive, with many rules and rituals. A child may participate in multigroup activities—a "Y" gymnastics class, a Little League team, a school dramatic club, and a neighborhood gang—all with different rules of organization, different membership, and different rituals.

Peer Influences. The peer-group experience contributes in a number of ways to the social development of the middle-years child.

INDEPENDENCE. The neighborhood clubroom or the school playground provides an early testing ground for childhood independence. While parental support and supervision are not far away, the child must respond to unfamiliar rules and situations without parental intervention.

SELF-CONCEPT. Through peer-group activities a child develops a self-concept. Psychological research dealing with popularity and self-esteem shows a correlation between negative peer evaluation and poor self-concept (14). Children who are not able to develop chum relationships and enter into peer-group activities, either because of lack of opportunity or because of personality drawbacks, feel like outsiders and do not fit easily into the mainstream of society in later life. They may turn to antisocial activities in order to find a feeling of belongingness or may become "loners" with few social outlets. Children who are not accepted by their peers should at this early period be given necessary emotional support to overcome their feelings of inadequacy so that they can develop affiliative relationships.

Peer-group interaction provides children with honest feedback on how they measure up to each other from the standpoint of personality and status. One of the hardest facts of life that the middle-years child has to face is the degree of selectivity that takes place in determining group membership. Although peer groups are often organized on a casual basis, with little thought given to rules and program activities, exclusivity of membership is a serious matter. Children look for such positive attributes in their friends as competence, social aggressiveness, wit, good looks, self-confidence, and friendliness. Children rejected from peer-group membership tend to show personality traits of anxiety, withdrawal behavior, and hostility.

Exclusion often evokes feelings of inferiority, which can lead to future alienation from peer society. More often, however, a number of rejectees get together and form their own club or gang and establish their own pecking order. Peer appraisals are usually devoid of subtlety, and children quickly learn where they stand by the nickname assigned them. Since even unkind evaluations are a form of recognition, a child will sometimes proudly accept his nickname ("Fatso") and show little resentment toward his friends, as long as they include him in the group.

Sometimes a child becomes a member of a group whose orientation is antithetical to his background. In such cases parents should weigh the degree of psychological advantage that membership represents against the negative aspects of the group's activities before separating the child from such a group.

PREPARATION FOR SOCIAL LIVING. The peer-group experience is the means by which the child prepares for societal life. The clubs and the gangs of the later years of middle childhood are founded on rigid codes of conduct which transmit values and standards while promising the child approval and acceptance if he conforms to group mores. Through the medium of group pressure the child gives up some of the more egocentric behavior patterns of former years in favor of compliance with group norms. While many groups of childhood emulate parental and societal standards of behavior, some deviate significantly, giving rise to conflicting allegiances. Studies show that children who identify with nurturant parents, parents who have by example provided them with strong models of suitable behavior, are more apt to resist contrasting group influences (11).

Parental Influences on Social Development. Despite the dichotomy in allegiance between the peer world and the world of "grown-ups," parents continue to exert a strong influence on the social development of the middle-years child.

By this age children have acquired more objectivity and become more aware of parental weaknesses and vulnerabilities. Although they are often embarrassed by their parents' "old-fashioned" ways, their desire to love and respect them is not far below the surface. Certainly children carry a strong feeling of family solidarity with them outside the home and quickly challenge any aspersions cast upon family members. Criticism of one's parent or sibling within the confines of the home is to be expected, but a friend's disparaging remarks about the same persons evoke harsh rebuke.

Through the identification process, parents become strong models for children during the middle years. Just as fond parents recount the accomplishments of their offspring, so also do children talk among themselves about the exciting occupations and activities of their parents.

PARENTAL SUPPORT. The child in his middle years is well on the road to independence and requires less supervision than previously; yet there continue to be many areas where parental support is essential. In the early grades the child is tentative in his social relationships and uncertain of appropriate behavior; he looks to parents for love and approval when faced with frustration or rejection by friends. His superego or conscience is in its formative stages, and parental attitudes play a strong role in determining moral development. Unfortunately, many children today are being short-changed in terms of the amount of time parents spend with them; by default, peer standards and television programs, which are often unwholesome, may exert more influence on moral development than do parents. Uri Bronfenbrenner, who made an extensive study of child-rearing practices in this country and in Russia, believes that much of the alienation and hostility that we may see in school-age children today can be traced to the failure of parents to spend sufficient time with their young (3).

ACADEMIC ENCOURAGEMENT. Parents also have a strong influence on children's academic motivation and achievement. Parents who assign a high priority to learning by joining a library, referring frequently to atlases, dictionaries, and encyclopedias in the home, and by reading to their children, as well as reading books for their own enjoyment, set an example for their children, who, in turn, are likely to develop respect for school and teachers.

Some parents, however, in their zeal to have their children do well academically may place undue emphasis on marks and performance. The child who is fearful of failure or of displeasing his parents becomes overly anxious and easily discouraged. While moderate anxiety levels have been found to increase learning motivation and achievement, excessive anxiety can lower performance levels.

School Influences. For the past few decades, public schools in this country have been under attack from many quarters for failing to meet the needs of children. Traditionalists have been concerned that with the movement away from language courses and subject-oriented curriculums, the public schools no longer provide a classical education. Conversely, those who favor a more "progressive" and child-centered curriculum accuse the schools of submission to a three-R's approach, and of failure to pay sufficient attention to the child's overall adjustment and mental health. The nationwide school desegregation program initiated in the sixties to overcome inequalities in educational opportunity has created sharp controversy over such issues as busing, funding for compensatory programs, teacher-pupil relationships, and class size, with little consensus evolving as to its effectiveness in improving learning skills and upgrading educationally disadvantaged children. In an evaluation of the program, mandated by the Civil Rights Act of 1964, a research team headed by James Coleman concluded that such factors as level of instruction, physical plant, class size, and curriculum enrichment, while important in themselves, do not have a crucial influence on student achievement. Social-class membership instead seemed to be the one variable that showed a consistent correlation with school performance (6). Children from upper- and middle-class homes showed higher achievement than those from lower-income homes; in other words, according to Coleman, and later, J. M. Stephens and Christopher Jencks, poor school performance is more directly the result of inequalities in economic standards and environmental conditions than of inequalities in educational opportunity.

Many educators, school administrators, mental health professionals, and parents today believe strongly that despite all of the educational innovations of the past fifteen years (team teaching, programed instructional techniques, language laboratories, and audiovisual aids, to name a few), our public schools are floundering. Many children leave elementary school not knowing how to read; truancy is a major problem in many school systems; and serious behavioral problems have reduced teachers in large measure to serving as hall monitors and custodians. Some researchers seriously question the wisdom of compulsory education. One writer, Ivan Illich, feels that school simply perpetuates the status quo and should therefore be abolished (15). Another, Paul Goodman, argues that formal schooling is unnecessary because most effective learning occurs incidentally (8). Such opinions echo the philosophy of A. S. Neill, the founder of a famous progressive school in England. Neill wrote in his book *Summerhill:* "My view is that a child is innately wise and realistic. If left to himself, without adult suggestion of any kind, he will develop as far as he is capable of developing" (23, p. 4). Christopher Jencks and his colleagues at the Harvard University Center for Educational Policy Research, in a study of the antecedents of adult success, found little relationship between adult success (as measured by income) and achievement in school (16).

Despite numerous negative evaluations of our public educational system, many children attend school happily and are in fact learning more than previous generations. Among the factors which lead to good school adjustment and which contribute to the socialization of the child are congenial classroom climate and sound teacher-pupil relationships.

CLASSROOM CLIMATE. Many conventional educators endorse a less formal school structure similar to the British Infant School model. They suggest an unregimented, noncompetitive type of classroom atmosphere that encourages children to learn because of the innate satisfactions derived from mastery and creativity. In such an "open classroom," children do not sit at their desks or tables all day; instead they are free to circulate to various learning centers within the room and interact with each other in small groups. Several children may form a group, for instance, to write a story together or solve a problem. The teacher in such a classroom spends more time working with individual children than addressing the whole class. Teachers find the open-classroom format more demanding because they must improvise materials and develop innovative teaching techniques. Not every teacher can adjust to the planned confusion characteristic of this type of setting. Children shuttle back and forth to various stations during the day, and do not as a matter of routine sit quietly in their seats. Nevertheless, many teachers have become enthusiastic converts to the open-classroom approach.

TEACHER-PUPIL RELATIONS. In the primary grades (first to third) the school is an extension of the home. The child's early experiences in the home are therefore generalized to the school situation and in many instances determine how he relates to the classroom setting and his teachers. Children who come from supportive and warm backgrounds will enter school with feelings of trust and acceptance; children who have not been fortunate in this respect may be suspicious of teachers and exhibit at school some of the hostility generated at home.

For the most part, children look forward to entrance into school and have positive attitudes toward it in the lower grades. As they progress, their initial enthusiasm seems to diminish. This is particularly true of children from lower-income families. Among the many possible reasons for this loss of interest, teacher attitudes and classroom management have significant impact. In general, children make a better school adjustment when their teachers respect them and reward their efforts. Children who are openly criticized by teachers and subjected to indifference and hostility are likely to do poorly in school.

While most children appreciate a firm teacher who brings order to their world, an authoritarian teacher who dominates the classroom may inhibit performance and adjustment. Children need to be able to express their feelings and hesitate to do so when they are overly controlled. In a classic study on this topic Kurt Lewin and two associates, Lippett and White, evaluated the behavior responses of an after-school club of eleven-year-old boys who were exposed variously to three different leadership styles—authoritarian, laissez-faire, and democratic (20). Trained observers in this study concluded that the authoritarian leadership produced either submissive or aggressive responses and a high degree of dependency upon the leader; that the laissez-faire approach failed to stimulate productive activity; and that the democratic style created more friendly relationships between club members, and higher morale and productivity.

As educators and mental health specialists become increasingly aware that most children experience stress in many aspects of their daily lives, more emphasis is being placed on "emotional learning" in our schools. A great variety of training materials have been prepared to assist teachers and guidance personnel to understand the psychological needs of children and to help them to deal effectively with their feelings. While such a program as the Besell and Palomares Human Development Program does not expect teachers to become psychologists, the authors do seek to enhance communication skills in the classroom, so that teachers can promote emotional as well as cognitive development. Underlying such psychoeducational programs, also known as affective learning, is the assumption that once children know how they feel and are encouraged to express and share their feelings with each other, they gain emotional strength and can concentrate on academic pursuits, rather than spending their energies in defensive maneuverings which interfere with learning (12). As early as 1952, Lawrence Kubie recognized the need for affective learning within the school structure when he wrote: "The child's fifth freedom is the right to know what he feels . . . this will require a new mores for our schools . . . which will enable young people from early years to understand and feel and put into words . . . things which go on inside them, thus ending the conspiracy of silence" (19, p. 146).

SEX EDUCATION. Learning about sex, biologically, behaviorally, and attitudinally, is an ongoing process which starts very early in life. Although Freud designates the middle years as a period of sexual latency, children from six through eleven are indeed interested in sex. The questions they ask about "the facts of life" and bodily organs indicate their curiosity, and the questions they avoid reflect their awareness of the taboo nature of the subject.

Children learn about sexual behavior in informal ways from their observation of parental relationships in the home. Parents who exhibit mutual respect and affection offer their children wholesome models of sexual behavior. By the same token children are influenced by parental responses toward such sex-related matters as privacy, masturbation, toilet habits, and bodily contact. Excessively constricted and "puritanical" attitudes on the part of primary caretakers engender feelings of guilt and anxiety in the child that may lead to inappropriate sexual inhibitions and may interfere with the development of normal sexual relationships.

Despite the fact that children today are growing up in a sexually permissive society, formal sex education in the schools is still a controversial issue. Parents opposed to such programs argue that the subject is best handled in the home. They are reluctant to trust teachers whose religious and moral views may not coincide with their own. Proponents of formal sex education point out, however, that children are exposed daily to sexual information and behavior in conversation with their peers, in watching television, and in reading books and magazines, all of which are beyond the control of most parents.

When schools do offer sex education programs, they begin in the early grades with simple biological facts pertaining to conception and birth and gradually through the years progress to more complex aspects of sexuality such as premarital sex, abortion, homosexuality, and venereal diseases.

ADJUSTMENT PROBLEMS OF CHILDHOOD

The period of middle childhood has been described as a time of pleasure and joy, unfettered by the concerns of "real life." Nevertheless, in view of the many hazards that children encounter at all ages, and the fact that the developmental demands of any period depend on the successful adjustment to earlier problems, it is hard to consider even the middle years as problem-free.

Learning Disabilities. In the course of formal schooling, most children learn what is expected of them in the prescribed time span. Some are not so fortunate because of learning difficulties. Among the causal factors underlying learning problems are mental retardation, emotional disturbance, physical handicaps, neurological disorders, and sociocultural pressures. The federal government recently estimated that there are 5 million school-age children with mental or physical handicaps in this country.

The term "learning disability" is sometimes used in a general sense to describe any number of school-related problems. As a diagnostic category it refers to a particular class of learning problems arising from specified causes. A New York State statute which conforms to federal descriptions identifies it as follows: "Specific learning disability means a disorder in one or more of the basic psychological processes involved in understanding or in using language, spoken or written, which may manifest itself in an imperfect ability to listen, think, speak, read, write, spell or do mathematical calculations. The term includes such conditions as perceptual handicaps, brain injury, minimal brain disfunction, dyslexia, and developmental aphasia. The term does not include learning problems which are primarily the result of visual, hearing, or motor handicaps, of mental retardation, of emotional disturbance, or of environmental, cultural, or economic disadvantage. A child who exhibits a discrepancy of 50% or more between expected achievement based on his intellectual ability and actual achievement, determined on an individual basis, shall be deemed to have a severe learning disability" (24).

Such refinements in terminology assume importance in terms of governmental funding policies for programs designed to offer special help and remediation to afflicted children. This statutory definition of learning disability thus limits the category to disabilities in learning which are traceable to neurologically based conditions rather than to anatomical, visual, auditory, intellectual, or environmental causes. Thus, a problem attributed to mental retardation, lack of motivation, maturational lag, poor or absent teaching, or lack of an enriching or encouraging home would technically not fall under the rubric of learning disability. The mechanisms that enable children to encode and decode, and to make sense of written and/or spoken letters, words, and sentences, are obstructed in children with learning disabilities. Letter combinations on a page may be reversed or appear garbled or meaningless; words and sentences may be heard correctly but not received or understood correctly by the appropriate brain mechanisms.

Various prescriptive teaching techniques have been used to help children overcome learning disabilities. Teaching strategies which focus on compensating for defective channels of learning by strengthening others have been successful. Kinesthetic methods, tracing letters and words, and limiting and repeating sounds have been found to be useful exercises.

Although many educators believe that children with learning disabilities require special education classes in school, others take the position that these children can be integrated into regular classes. The latter approach has been termed "mainstreaming." Under these circumstances the child attends regular classes but receives additional specialized tutoring at specified times during the school day. The benefits and detriments of mainstreaming require further study and research before a valid judgment of this approach can be made.

Mental Retardation. Mental retardation is usually first identified during middle childhood. While a small group of children in this category show marked retardation and severe limitation of intelligence, most retardates are mildly impaired and are considered educable or trainable. In the past, children whose IQs fell below a designated level (usually 70 or 75 IQ) were considered to be mentally retarded. Special classes, schools, and institutions were created for them, and placement was determined primarily by IQ. As scientists and educators have developed a better understanding of the phenomenon of retardation they have become more and more reluctant to use the IQ as the exclusive criterion. Children's IQ scores may be affected by physical, social, and emotional factors. Consequently the criteria for defining mental retardation have been broadened to include degree of adequacy of social and academic skills. Children who are truly mentally retarded reveal a marked and persistent impairment in all areas, including the ability to understand, to learn, and to adapt to social demands. They seek out younger children as playmates and prefer games typical of earlier developmental periods. Children who are thus affected remain retarded throughout life, persistently manifesting the impairment of intellectual ability needed for coping with and solving life's situations.

The degree of retardation, whether mild or severe, is important not only in schooling but also in terms of expectations for adult living. The *profoundly retarded* child has the lowest IQ (below 25) and mental age level, and is not expected to benefit from academically oriented teaching. He will require regular care and supervision throughout his life. The *moderately retarded* child with an IQ that may range from 25 to 50 is considered trainable. This child is not capable of independent living but can be taught certain academic skills and can learn to perform some simple tasks, making him eligible for employment in sheltered workshops. *Mildly or educably retarded* children make up the greater proportion (75 to 80 percent) of retarded children. They show a relatively mild impairment of intellect (IQ of 50 to 75) and usually attend school. Obviously the higher the IQ within this category, the less the impairment in functioning. Children at the lower end of the 50–75 IQ range can be expected to encounter more difficulty in and out of school. The educably retarded child is able to learn to read, write, and do simple arithmetic computations, although at a lower level of proficiency and at a slower rate than the child of average intelligence. As he grows into adulthood and fits into the work world he is confronted with fewer formal intellectual requirements and his deficiencies become less manifest.

When children who are educably retarded are no longer faced with formal schooling, most of them are viewed as average and normal adults.

The causes of mental retardation have been traced to genetic endowment, to constitutional factors in prenatal development (maternal health problems), to injury sustained during the birth process, and to injury of the brain resulting from disease and illness during the early years of life. In some instances no discernible or clear cause can be found.

School Phobia. A problem encountered occasionally by parents of middle-years children is the reluctance of the child to go to school. The incidence of stomach pain, headache, nausea, or general malaise appears to fluctuate with school-related incidents. Examinations, taunting classmates, athletic ineptitude, angry teachers, uncompleted homework, and a multitude of similar conditions appear to spark the child's unwillingness to go to school.

In most cases, the child's absence from school is temporary. In some instances, however, resistance to school is intense; the child exhibits fear and foreboding, and no reasons for these feelings can be uncovered which are commensurate with the amount of anxiety the child displays. All attempts at coercion, reasoning, and pleading prove unsuccessful. The child refuses to attend school, and forceful persuasion only intensifies the somatic symptoms. When the child is permitted to remain home, his complaints usually subside until it is time to return to school.

There have been a number of explanations for school phobia. Some authorities see this behavior as a neurotic reaction stemming from the displacement onto the school of unconscious conflicts originating in the early family life of the child. Fear of parental punishment may become fear of school or teacher, or fear of punishment for academic failure or transgression. The basic fear is that of parent rejection. Another related explanation views the parent and child as enmeshed in a symbiotic dependency; the parent is unconsciously reluctant to let the child go, and the child wishes to satisfy the unconscious desire of the parent as the way of ensuring parental love. Other theorists emphasize the reality of the school as a major factor in school phobia. The child is literally afraid of failure in school and its attendant teacher disapproval and the loss of self-esteem. There may be elements in the school situation which are associated with earlier feared experiences, objects, or people.

The child with a temporary reluctance to go to school may be permitted to stay home for a day. The phobic child, however, requires systematic and deeply based approaches such as psychotherapy, counseling, and conditioning techniques. Usually the child is able to return to school in a fairly short period of time, although a few cases require prolonged treatment.

Behavior Disorders. Children obviously become troublesome at home and at school when they display difficult behavior. Conduct disorders are particularly significant in the classroom where the disruptive child interferes with the learning of his classmates, intrudes on their rights, and becomes a source of contagious misbehavior. Behavior disorders may be mild and environmentally stimulated or they may be symptomatic of serious psychological maladjustment. Some children become persistent conduct problems because the peer code dictates unruly behavior; others suffer from a sense of inadequacy or rejection and "act out" their unresolved conflicts. Environmentally stimulated disorders are usually transitory because most children modify their behavior as conditions change and they mature.

The types of behavior disorders that stem from psychological conflicts in the child, or from certain neurological afflictions, are more serious. The child who has developed strong hostile feelings toward parents and has decided that all adults are punitive comes to school with a chip on his shoulder and is ready to explode at any request or admonition. The child who feels lost and neglected may find that he can be the center of attention by stealing, fighting, or engaging in other antisocial acts.

Treatment depends upon the nature of the problem, its causes, and the theoretical orientation from which it is viewed. The child with deep-seated problems requires a therapeutic treatment approach. Children with conduct disorders unfortunately do not respond as readily to psychological intervention and often become the juvenile delinquents of later childhood.

7
Adolescence

As the child completes his adjustment to the problems of the middle years, at approximately ten years of age, he has accomplished a great deal. He has come to reasonably good terms with himself, his parents and brothers and sisters, the community between his home and the local school, and his friends and age-mates. At this time, however, he is facing a period of major change, requiring new adjustments. In a relatively short span of years he will hardly recognize his physical self; he will need to readjust his relationships to parents, other adults, age-mates, and young people of the opposite sex; he will have to find a new understanding of himself; he will have to develop goals that will guide him for the rest of his life. This time of transition is adolescence.

Adolescence may be formally defined as the period of development between childhood and adulthood, characterized by specific physiological changes and bracketed by chronological age as specified by each society and culture (in Western culture, usually the "teen" years). It is a period of growth in which young men and women achieve physical and intellectual maturity and during which a number of unique developmental tasks are worked out. Among these tasks of adolescence are the following:

1. Achieving independence from parents
2. Molding a clear and acceptable self-concept and achieving a sense of identity
3. Establishing a masculine or feminine identification and arriving at a satisfactory definition of that role
4. Crystallizing a set of values as a guide to living with other people
5. Developing social relationships with peers and adults
6. Clarifying academic and vocational goals

These tasks will be discussed in the sections on personality and social development.

PHYSICAL DEVELOPMENT

Physical adolescence begins with a period of growth and maturation called *pubescence* or sometimes *preadolescence*. It culminates about two years later in *puberty*, the time of life when the body is ready for procreation. It is at puberty that the girl gets her first menstrual period, the menarche, and the boy shows sperm in the urine.

Growth Spurt. One of the most readily apparent characteristics of early adolescence is the sudden increase in height. Growth spurt is the result of a series of complex interactions among some of the endocrine glands: the pituitary, the thyroid, the adrenals, and the gonads (testes and ovaries). The pituitary gland, often referred to as the "master gland," releases a growth hormone that initiates the rapid increase in height. Skeletal and muscular growth proceeds in a regular sequence during the growth spurt. The head, feet, and hands mature before full trunk length and breadth are reached. By the end of adolescence, complete fusion of bone and skeletal structure is achieved.

The pituitary also secretes a hormone which increases the size and activity of the gonads, which in turn causes a slackening of the growth spurt with a subsequent leveling off of the growth process.

During the growth spurt the internal organs, including the heart and lungs, develop toward mature proportions. Only the brain, which has already reached 95 percent of its total weight by this time, remains untouched by the growth spurt.

VARIATIONS IN GROWTH RATE. The growth spurt varies widely from individual to individual in terms of age of onset, duration, and extent. Girls usually start their growth acceleration about two years ahead of boys. They reach a maximum rate of growth at about twelve years of age, whereas boys, on the average, reach their peak at fourteen. Growth curve charts for age-mates during this rapid growth period show considerable overlapping between individual boys and girls. Growth then slows down and continues until full mature height is reached at the end of the seventeenth year for most girls and several years later for boys (8).

Although girls on the average are heavier and taller than boys of the same age during the growth spurt interval, boys eventually overtake girls in height and weight. By the end of adolescence boys as a group also surpass girls in degree of strength because of their greater muscular development, higher blood pressure levels, metabolic capacity, and larger heart and lungs.

ASYNCHRONOUS GROWTH. Prepubertal boys and girls often feel awkward because of the unfamiliarity of their quickly changing bodies. Contributing to this sense of awkwardness is the unevenness of body growth: the upper part of the face lengthens before the lower part, the feet mature before the legs, and the legs before the trunk. Despite this unevenness of development, the adolescent functions well in many activities that require good coordination. Many young people of this age excel in athletics, dancing, repair of machinery, and playing a musical instrument.

Secondary Sex Characteristics. In addition to muscular and skeletal development, pubescent adolescents change in other ways that make them look more and more like adults. The "baby fat" is replaced by a solid and sturdy body structure. The asynchrony terminates and the various parts of the body fall into a harmonious pattern. A further developmental pattern is the emergence of the secondary sex characteristics, or sex-identifying qualities, of the individual. This process is under the control of hormones secreted by the gonads, or sex glands. In both boys and girls, pubic and underarm hair begins to show itself and gradually becomes fuller. The skin becomes coarser, the sweat glands more active, and acne may develop. In boys, facial hair makes its appearance; chest hair comes later in adolescence. The growth of the larynx is responsible for the voice breaks in boys. The penis and the scrotum show marked increase in size. In girls the breasts begin to grow, the nipples become more prominent, and the pelvis enlarges. The body fat of the maturing girl gives her a rounded appearance, whereas boys begin to look muscular.

Puberty. When adolescents reach the crest of the period of accelerated growth, and when the development of the secondary sex characteristics is well under way, they move into a further stage of physical development. This stage, called puberty, is marked by the appearance of the menarche, the beginning of menstruation, in girls. In boys the clinical evidence of puberty can be found by the appearance of spermatozoa, the male seed for procreation, in the urine.

Although it is frequently assumed that the capacity for reproduction is achieved at puberty, the evidence indicates that true sexual maturity is not reached until one to three years later. Usually the beginning menstrual cycle is irregular and incapable of bringing forth ripe ova, or eggs, for reproductive purposes. Ejaculation in boys of this period reveals negligible amounts of spermatozoa, and most of these are nonactive. As a result, the possibility of becoming pregnant or of inducing pregnancy among youngsters at this stage of development is unlikely, although certainly not impossible.

Trends in Maturation and Growth. Our present culture has prolonged the period of adolescence by requiring more years of schooling and by legally deferring entrance into the labor market. Nevertheless, it is a biological fact that boys and girls are leaving childhood at an earlier age than prior generations. In girls, the average age of menarche has dropped approximately 2½ to 3½ years during the past century. Improved nutritional standards and better medical care all play a part in this phenomenon.

Adolescents today are also taller than their counterparts in previous generations. This trend toward greater height has persisted over the past hundred years. However, the U.S. National Center for Health Statistics, which has studied 20,000 American children from infancy through adolescence, has recently reported that the trend toward bigger Americans has either ceased or is tapering off. Whereas children have, in the past, increased in height about a half-inch per decade, the young people studied recently showed little, if any, increase over those of ten years ago. At the present time the average American adult male is slightly over 5 feet 9 inches, the female 5 feet 4 inches in height, which represents an increase of 4 inches in one hundred years (15).

MENTAL DEVELOPMENT

Mental development is, of course, a continual process. The results of that development depend on the constant interaction of inborn endowment, maturational unfolding, and the effects of environment and experience. Prior to adolescence, the child has been testing, experiencing, and refining his mental skills. Nevertheless, his mental ability is not yet fully developed, just as his body is not yet fully mature. Intellectual maturity, like physical maturity, is reached in late adolescence. This does not mean that the individual reaches the peak of learning at that age; it means that the anatomical components of mental development—the brain, nerves, and sense organs—have fully matured. Just as a late adolescent who has the muscles and bone growth necessary to run fast may not choose to join the track team, so an individual who has achieved full development of his mental abilities may not be attracted to pursuits that utilize his full intellectual powers. Later in life he may decide to embark on a career requiring the maximum use of his intellect. Thus, the peak of learning would be realized after intellectual maturity had been reached.

Cognitive Growth. In Piaget's scheme of cognitive development, the child at about age twelve passes from the stage of concrete operations (concrete thinking) to the stage of formal operations (abstract thinking). This means that the early adolescent is increasingly able to see alternative approaches to issues and problems. He is now bringing abstract thinking to bear on issues that heretofore he has seen as single-dimensional (6). Thus he can spend countless hours on seemingly fruitless semantic exercises such as whether or not there is sound if a tree falls in a forest with no one near to hear it fall.

Exposure to New Ideas. At the same time the adolescent's cognitive capacity is increasing, his world is expanding. Being older and more mobile, he is likely to meet many different types of people whose ideas and conclusions are at variance with those of his parents, his teachers, and other influential adults. Partly because he is refining his cognitive skills and partly because he is working toward independence and trying to formulate his own attitudes and values, the adolescent begins to raise questions and argue with adults and peers. Religion, politics, sex, television, sports, films—all become topics for controversy.

Intellectualization. The increasing mental maturity of the adolescent affects other facets of his life. There is increasing use, for example, of intellectualization as a defense mechanism. Confronted with many potentially anxiety-provoking people and situations, the adolescent rushes into talk. The intellectual discussion and the abstract argument become the focus of attention, and in this way the young person avoids facing the underlying issues (girls, boys, aggression). It is less difficult, and even intellectually stimulating, to discuss war and aggression between nations than to acknowledge and cope with the angry, frustrating feelings that lie within. It is easier to discuss sexual morality than to face the dilemma posed by a real boy-girl relationship.

Introspective Thinking. As his intellect develops, the teen-ager becomes involved in the search for identity and is very concerned with how he feels about himself and how others view him. Egocentric and introspective, he spends much time analyzing himself, thinking about himself, and comparing himself with others. As a result, self-consciousness becomes more pronounced at this time. Also, as a result of his introspection, the adolescent's self-image keeps changing, causing fluctuations in moods and sensitivity.

PERSONALITY DEVELOPMENT

Personality, or the complex of characteristics and tendencies that make a person unique, evolves slowly throughout the growing years. Each age and stage of life provides forces that act on the child and help to shape his personality.

Factors Affecting Adolescent Personality. The personality development of the adolescent rests upon a number of interrelated factors.

PREVIOUS SELF-IMAGE. Much depends on how the personality has developed up to this time. The child of the middle years has a view of himself which, though certainly modifiable, affects the way he handles his life in adolescence. This view of himself includes an estimate of his self-worth and of his physical, mental, and social assets and liabilities. It encompasses his attitudes toward others and toward achievement, school, and work.

THE STATE OF SOCIETY. Extremely influential in the personality development of the adolescent is the historical present—all that is going on in society at the time. Thus, the political climate, the state of the economy, and the degree of drug usage present the adolescent with dilemmas and conflicts. They become obstacles in the resolution of developmental tasks on the one hand and practical problems to be solved on the other.

THE PHYSICAL SELF. It is one thing to say that, statistically, the early adolescent starts his or her growth spurt anywhere from ten to fourteen years of age. It is quite another thing to actually be a small, undeveloped junior high school boy studying alongside one's taller, fairly well built age-mates. The actual facts of physical development determine the adolescent's feelings about himself as a person. Therefore, personality growth can be hindered or facilitated by physique and physical appearance.

Studies of early- and late-maturing boys reveal that early maturers tend to be more popular and self-confident, whereas late starters are likely to remain on the fringes of groups, show less self-assuredness, and experience more tension and problems in adjustment (19, 10). The picture for girls is not as clear. In the past, early-maturing girls tended to show an out-of-step reaction and some difficulty in adjustment (5). They felt gawky and awkward in the presence of their female contemporaries who had not yet begun to grow. Their "differentness" was even more pronounced when they were among their male schoolmates of the same age, who normally lag behind girls by two years in beginning the growth spurt. However, this tendency seems to be disappearing as society is accepting a newer and wider role for women. Inasmuch as there is a high correlation between the growth spurt and the onset of puberty, these early postpubertal girls attract the attention of older male adolescents and the envy and admiration of their less precocious sisters.

The acquiring of secondary sex characteristics affects the adolescent's self-esteem, attitude toward school, relationships to peers, and, of course, his behavior. He is rapidly developing the capability of sexual reproduction with all of the personal and social implications of that capability.

THE PEER GROUP. The adolescent uses the peer group as a sounding board (adults generally, and parents particularly, are too "out of it"), as an arena for trying out the adultlike self and behavior, as support for his growing autonomy and independence from his parents, and as a source of values he can find acceptable. Thus, the peer group sets the standards for dress, behavior, language, and leisure activity. As a result of these pressures some personality characteristics are modified, others inhibited, and still others emerge.

Tasks in Personality Development. At the beginning of this chapter there is a list of the developmental tasks of adolescence. The first four of these relate to personality development.

ACHIEVING INDEPENDENCE. This task is frequently the source of much conflict between adolescent and parent. As the young person moves from early to late adolescence, he assumes an increasing degree of adultlike, independent behavior. This behavior often fails to meet parental standards and rules, particularly with regard to choice of friends, activities, hours, clothes, and language. The problem is complicated by the fact that the child is somewhat ambivalent about growing up and becoming independent. While reaching for independence there is still a need for the safety and comfort of being cared for. The parent is also ambivalent about the child's growing independence. It is the hope of every parent that the child will eventually be able to stand on his own two feet. Nevertheless, the parent finds the child's growing up and growing away a painful process, carrying with it a feeling of being abandoned and a reminder of his own or her own advancing age. This ambivalence on the part of both parent and child has been termed dual ambivalence.

American society presents the young person with many obstacles to independence. This difficult transition is facilitated in families that follow patterns characterized as democratic, in which children are encouraged to participate in discussions regarding standards, rules, and behavior. Children from democratic homes are likely to develop personality characteristics such as self-confidence, high self-esteem, and the ability to make decisions. Consequently they achieve an appropriate degree of autonomy with relative ease. Parents who rely on arbitrary and authoritarian rule-setting or who abandon the parental role by excessive permissiveness or neglect create a milieu in which it is hard for children to achieve genuine independence (14).

THE SEARCH FOR IDENTITY. The adolescent is constantly asking himself "Who am I?" The question is asked directly at times, indirectly at others. The answer is often sought in the mirror. "What is the physical me? Can I change it? Do I wish to change it?" The young person tries the sound of a different name, as if by changing the label, the contents will more closely fit the elusive, ideal self. He looks at his present self and draws inferences about his future self. "If I'm scared of girls now," the boy may think, "then I'll probably never be able to get a girl interested in me." Boys and girls constantly test out their developing values against those of society, parents, and peers. They then question their own ability to adhere to the values in which they profess to believe.

Since early childhood, the child has given some thought to what he wants to be when he grows up. Now, in adolescence, he *is* growing up and will soon have to make a decision. Work takes on a greater import as a definer of identity. He now feels his future work will figure largely in what he will *be*. Moreover, his concern is not simply: "What career shall I choose?" from the bewildering array of vocations that everyone seems to think is available to the adolescent. It is also: "Can I make it?" The adolescent senses his lack of age and experience, and he knows some of his limitations. This knowledge is a basis for much anxiety as he searches for a life work.

The sense of identity of the adolescent at any particular time is thus an amalgam of what he is, what he thinks he is, what parents and others think he is, and the ideal self which he uses as a measuring rod. Eventually he will acquire an adult self-concept and a sureness of footing on the path of life, relatively secure in himself and what he can do.

ESTABLISHING A PSYCHOSEXUAL IDENTIFICATION. The child at adolescence must establish a masculine or feminine identification. This task, which is part of the search for identity, is distinct from, although obviously related to, acceptance of the facts of physical maleness or femaleness. The adolescent must come to terms with what it means to be a man or woman in his or her society.

In the past, sex role distinctions were relatively clear. Males were the breadwinners, strong, adventurous, and brave, and they were permitted a degree of sexual freedom denied to females. Women, stereotypically, were homemakers, shy, tender, and emotional, and financially and socially dependent upon men. Deviations such as homosexuality or bisexuality were considered perversions to be shunned.

These stereotypes have been gradually changing, making psychosexual identifications more difficult. The feminist movement has opened doors for women that were previously closed, including wider occupational choices. Personality characteristics once considered unfeminine are now acceptable. Girls are not considered "too forward" today when they take the initiative in telephoning boys, and "Dutch treat" dates are now common. Although the masculine stereotype has undergone less change, there is currently a wider acceptance of the sensitive and child-oriented male. The growth of the gay movement, which is working toward an acceptance of homosexuality as a psychosexual choice, has further added to the complexity of this developmental task.

CRYSTALLIZING A SET OF VALUES. In the course of their development, most children function within a series of different ideological frameworks. At any particular time, the accepted values may differ significantly from home to school, from neighborhood to society. Moreover, there may be a contradiction between the stated accepted value and the manifest behavior. For example, lying and cheating are called wrong, but the very individuals who emphasize this may themselves lie and cheat.

The adolescent, as he grows toward intellectual maturity, is increasingly able to analyze social issues and is quick to hold up the shortcomings and contradictions of society as evidence of the hypocrisy of the establishment. In his search for alternative values, he may gravitate toward religious and quasi-religious movements such as the Eastern religions and philosophies, mysticism, fundamental asceticism, and Transcendental Meditation. He may become politically active in organizations working for specific causes. He may reject the traditional goals and conventional life styles of his parents or society and live in a commune or move to other countries.

Changes in time and focus of social concerns see changes in the manifestations of the adolescent's search for a stable set of values. The great majority of student activists of the 1960s graduated and went on to work or to graduate study, and campus demonstrations are no longer a major characteristic of college life. Although there was still concern with societal problems, college youth of the late 1970s appeared to be more preoccupied with getting good grades, gaining admission to graduate and professional schools, getting a job, and earning a living.

SOCIAL DEVELOPMENT

The changing social relationships of the adolescent are attributable in large part to the physical and sexual transformations that initiate and accompany this stage of development. These changing relationships occur between the teen-ager and his parents and between the teen-ager and other adults, both in terms of the amount of time spent together and the nature and quality of the association. In addition, new peer relationships with both the same and the opposite sex must be established. The age at which young adolescents begin to explore and develop these more mature social relationships is, to a great extent, culturally determined.

Adolescence "Created" and "Discovered." In our culture, adolescence has only recently emerged as a socially significant stage of life. In earlier times it was assumed that adulthood started at puberty when the young person took on additional responsibilities on the farm, in the mine, or in the factory, and then entered into early marriage. As modern industrialized society and social conditions created socioeconomic changes in the late nineteenth century, the young were less and less needed in the work force. As a result, multitudes of young people were fed into thousands of mushrooming secondary schools (12). In this way children of this age group became distinguishable from their younger brothers and sisters and from adult society in terms of social role and societal expectations (2). Thus, "adolescence" was produced by society and then "discovered" by G. Stanley Hall when he wrote his comprehensive study in 1904 (7).

The present-day adolescent must define his social role in this vague and ambiguous in-between period, while preparing to assume an adult role a few years hence. Whereas the middle-years child is very much a part of the family unit, the early adolescent is pulling away from family ties. Parents of adolescents express surprise and hurt as their teen-agers ease themselves out of family picnics and vacation trips, erect a wall of privacy and exclusion, and even refuse to take responsibility for family chores. They miss the mellow moments when they and their children used to sit together and talk and share experiences and feelings. Knowing so little about their teen-agers' daily lives and finding their own advice unwelcome, parents feel great concern that their children will fall prey to the dangers that lurk beyond the confines of the home—physical violence, drugs, and premature, potentially harmful sexual involvement. Young people in turn see parental apprehension as a form of intrusion and mistrust of their judgment. This intensifies conflict and increases the distance between parents and adolescents.

The Generation Gap. While the rift and abrasiveness between generations has always existed to some degree, there is evidence that the conflict is greater today than in the past. Social change is proceeding at a more rapid pace; customs and acceptable life styles and behavior are shifting more quickly. The lessons of personal experience which parents have always felt able to pass on to their young become less pertinent as guidelines for living in the present world.

Indeed, anthropologists point out that the degree of tension between the generations in any society is closely related to the rapidity and complexity of social and technological change. Adolescents in simple societies with rigid rules and fixed social structures move into postpuberty with almost no "storm and stress" (13). In these societies the personal and social roles and relationships are clearly defined, and life proceeds with relative continuity from generation to generation. In modern societies, such as the United States today, the young person is faced with an array of choices as to social role, relationships, and allegiances. Furthermore, in our age of rapid acceleration, by the time a child who is born today graduates from college, the world will have increased its fund of scientific knowledge many times over (18). The gap between the adult and soon-to-be-adult world will continue to widen.

Peer Relationships. In early or preadolescence, at about junior high school age, some major changes in peer relationships occur as boys and girls become preoccupied with their bodies and their appearance. These body changes are extremely sensitive concerns, and are discussed (and even then cautiously) only among members of the same sex. There is a great deal of conjecture and sharing of information regarding physical characteristics. Because girls mature before boys, they begin this same-sex grouping concerned with the new adolescent feelings while boys of their age are still involved in the activities of middle-year interest. When the transition starts, the play groups of earlier childhood realign themselves somewhat on the basis of maturational development, the less precocious members being by-passed by their more pubescent age-mates.

During the early adolescent years the sexes do not intermingle in any real sense. It is a time for youngsters to learn how to get along with members of their own sex. They confide in each other and receive emotional support from the commonality of their experiences and feelings. They carry on endless telephone and street group conversations about anything and everything. Girls, because of their earlier maturation, are more interested in boys than are boys of the same age interested in girls. Thus, girl-groups, although they may not mix or associate with boys in the heterosexual sense, talk about appearance, sexual attractiveness, and, of course, boys. Later in adolescence, boys and girls begin to "hang out" together.

Crushes. As parents are displaced by peers in terms of influence, other adults may play selectively important roles. Special teachers, camp counselors, adult relatives or neighbors, and older adolescents become objects of admiration or even of infatuation. At times these attachments affect the choices made by adolescents regarding school,

SOCIAL DEVELOPMENT

vocation, and the like. Frequently, crushes are kept secret and are revealed only in a treasured diary. Such secrets are sometimes shared with members of the inner circle.

Sexual Patterns. In later adolescence when group members begin to feel more confident, they may pair off with members of the opposite sex and engage in sexual experimentation. Groups grow smaller and double dating becomes popular. The privacy of a car or a corner of a park provides sufficient seclusion for sexual intimacy. While sexual patterns of behavior are diverse, depending on family influence and social class mores, recent generations of adolescents are, in general, more sexually active than prior ones, beginning at an earlier age (11). This new sexual freedom among teen-agers does not imply rampant promiscuity. Sexual intimacy can signify fidelity to a particular partner, mutual affection, and even intent to marry (17). Nevertheless, whether culturally or biologically determined, boys show stronger sex drives and are more sexually active than girls during early adolescence. Their need for commitment is, therefore, not as great. Consequently, young girls often suffer deep emotional trauma when sexual urgency is mistaken for strong attachment. It has been said that young boys sometimes play with love for sex, and young girls play with sex for love.

Two serious problems associated with the greater sexual freedom among adolescents in this country are the high rate of teen-age pregnancy and the increased incidence of venereal disease.

TEEN-AGE PREGNANCY. Despite the fact that we are living in what is considered to be an open society with birth control information readily available, teen-age boys and girls do not in general take adequate precautionary measures to prevent pregnancy.

Most adolescent pregnancies occur because of (1) insufficient sex education, (2) fear on the part of both partners of destroying the spontaneity of the sex act through use of birth control methods, (3) impulsive sex behavior without thought of consequences, and (4) society's more liberal view of unmarried motherhood in recent years. The high rate of repeated pregnancies among teen-age girls also supports the theory that some girls have a conscious or unconscious desire to become pregnant, hoping that the birth of the child will fulfill some unmet needs for love and dependency.

VENEREAL DISEASE. The rate of venereal disease, especially gonorrhea, has reached epidemic proportions in this country, the fifteen-to nineteen-year-old category being one of the main groups to contract it (3). Health professionals are also reporting for this age group a rise in cases of other, less-well-known venereal diseases such as herpes progenitalis, trichomiasis, and hemophilus vaginalis. The substitution of oral contraception for the condom, resulting in less prophylactic protection, along with earlier and more frequent sexual activity, has in large part accounted for the increased incidence in venereal diseases. More widespread sex education by schools, parents, and community agencies is needed to combat ignorance and reduce the heavy physical and psychological price that adolescents are paying for their newly found sexual freedom.

ADJUSTMENT PROBLEMS OF ADOLESCENCE

Since the time of G. Stanley Hall, theoreticians and others studying or working with adolescents have considered this period a time of "sturm und drang." Because all adolescents are faced with enormous changes and have many choices forced upon them, the terms "adolescence" and "maladjustment" were considered to be almost synonomous. However, although some young people do suffer enduring psychological difficulty in adolescence, most encounter only temporary problems and make the adjustments fairly smoothly.

Depression and Suicide. Some of the problems of adolescent adjustment stem directly from physical changes. The more significant adjustment problems, however, result less from the physical changes themselves than from the young person's emotional reaction to them. It is not uncommon for the adolescent to exhibit mood swings as he experiences feelings of confusion, helplessness, and hopelessness. Thus he shifts very quickly from being happy to being sad. At times, the adolescent becomes depressed. Such depression, although deeply felt, is for most young people of short duration. For others, however, the disturbance continues for long periods of time and constitutes a severe adjustment problem of adolescence.

The depressed individual is apathetic and immobilized, and gets little, if any, gratification from life. He sees himself as alone and powerless in a world of forces that overwhelm him. At times, the depth and severity of the depression lead the young person to believe there is no way out other than death. Suicide is, in fact, one of the most frequent causes of death in adolescence. It has become a serious enough problem to warrant the attention of community groups and social agencies who set up "hot lines" and prevention centers. One study of adolescent suicide (9) suggests that those who contemplate suicide are youngsters who have had emotional problems from early childhood and who suffer greater than usual stress during the adolescent period. Unable to cope with the mounting problems of this age, they begin to withdraw from social relationships and finally reach "the end of hope."

Anorexia Nervosa. Anorexia nervosa, or loss of appetite in the absence of organic disease, is a disorder of adolescence which is far from common but striking enough to mention. This condition is found almost exclusively among girls, who become obsessed with the idea that they are overweight and need to diet. The refusal of food, which the victim finds extremely distasteful, becomes so severe at times as to require hospitalization and intravenous feeding. The cause of this disorder, which is sometimes fatal, appears to be psychological, perhaps of psychosexual origin (16).

School Problems. Many emotional problems in adolescence find their expression in the academic area; one of these is underachievement, another is dropping out of school.

UNDERACHIEVEMENT. Although underachievement may be caused by a learning disability that has gone undetected in the earlier grades, in adolescence it is often due to a shift of interest from school to social activities. During the teen years sexual interests and peer activities often take priority over academic learning. School just doesn't seem to have much value in the "here and now" for some young people, and it is that here and now that counts most in the adolescent's world. Underachievement can also occur when a child has hostile feelings toward his parents. The process is usually unconscious. The young person hits back at the parent for real or imagined pressures, punishments, or other relationship difficulties by doing poorly in school. In effect he is saying through his behavior: "I may suffer for what I am doing, but my mother [or parents] will suffer more, and it's worth it."

THE DROPOUT. In some instances the academic problems derive from a lack of agreement between what the young person sees as his or her needs and what the school provides. There may be an inflexible curriculum, an insensitive school staff, or inadequate resources because of budgetary restrictions. In an extreme reaction, the adolescent leaves school before completing the requirements for a diploma. It is overly simplistic to lay the cause at the school's doorstep. Likewise, it misses the complexity of the problem to blame the child. Some studies report that dropping out is the end result of many other problems, some of which can be traced to much earlier periods in the child's life. Socioeconomic factors and family problems may play a role. By high school age many of the seeds for poor school adjustment have been sown. These include low self-esteem, past scholastic failures, low aspirations, and patterns of deviant behavior. There is some evidence that the personality problems of the dropout do not worsen as a result of leaving school. There is a greater incidence of delinquency among this group, but this characteristic was usually present before the time of dropping out (1).

School dropouts experience occupational and economic consequences. Young people from some minority groups, including blacks and Puerto Ricans, often find it difficult to get jobs. The causes are, in part, traceable to the fact that many of these youths have dropped out of school with no marketable skills. In their frustration and despair, they may turn to drugs and delinquency, becoming both psychologically and socially maladjusted.

Drug Abuse. The use of drugs to uplift the spirits and overcome physical discomfort is as old as mankind. The widespread use of drugs by the young is, however, a fairly recent phenomenon in Western society, especially for middle-class youth, and has become a major cause of intergenerational conflict. Ironically, adult society has provided a precedent for the youthful drug culture by its own pervasive reliance on tranquilizers, stimulants, pain-relievers, alcohol, and tobacco. While some adolescents may think that they are rebelling against the adult establishment by indulging in drugs, they are actually imitating their elders.

Most teen-agers are not drug addicts or alcoholics. However, much experimentation is going on in this age group and at earlier ages. Peer group affiliation and parental examples seem to play a role in influencing the susceptible teen-ager as to both choice of substance and degree of use or abuse. Children are more likely to become heavy drinkers or regular smokers, for example, if a parent or close friend drinks or smokes. There also seems to be a correlation between family instability and drug use; adolescents who are trying to escape an unpleasant home life are more apt to turn to drugs.

Tobacco, alcohol, and marijuana are the most popular drugs in use by adolescents today. Alcohol consumption has been increasing. Although smoking among boys has abated somewhat, there is an upsurge on the part of girls despite the fact that both sexes are well aware of the physical consequences. Unfortunately, most adolescents are not really convinced of the addictive nature of tobacco and feel they will be able to break the habit at will. Adolescents smoke cigarettes, consume alcohol, and use marijuana for many reasons: to satisfy curiosity, to be sociable, to overcome mild anxiety, and to feel more grown-up. Fortunately, only a small minority of adolescents use narcotics. These individuals on hard drugs are usually trying to overcome despair by escaping into oblivion.

Juvenile Delinquency. Depending on residence, children over seven years of age and under sixteen or eighteen are classified as juvenile delinquents when they commit legally recognized criminal acts. Furthermore, truancy, running away, and incorrigibility on the part of juveniles constitute delinquent conduct.

Some factors contributing to juvenile delinquency are:

1. Longstanding history of parental neglect and emotional deprivation
2. Harsh and inconsistent discipline with unrewarding adult relationships
3. Exposure to the disorganization and anonymity of inner-city life
4. Disruption of family ties as a result of social and geographical mobility, divorce, or death
5. Drug dependence with constant need for money to support the habit
6. Dropping out of school
7. Progressively poor social, academic, and emotional adjustment from childhood on into adolescence

Some writers distinguish between social or sociological delinquency and delinquency stemming from psychological and personality problems. The first is represented by the type of act that is often part of neighborhood or gang behavior. For example, counterculture youths may steal from department stores, believing that the establishment should be "ripped off" or taken advantage of. The second type of juvenile crime is related to personality problems and defects within the child. In such instances, the delinquent act is a behavioral expression of psychological difficulties such as hostility to parents, feelings of inadequacy, or an inability to develop a level of conscience strong enough to fit in with the accepted norms of society.

Many states have separate juvenile courts designed to protect and rehabilitate youthful offenders. However, in the light of the upsurge in juvenile crime, state legislatures are now beginning to enact more stringent legislation pertaining to juvenile behavior.

Unfortunately, law enforcement agents and social agencies, while recognizing the sharp increase in juvenile crime in recent years, have had little success in curbing juvenile delinquency, although many approaches have been tried (4). One reason for this lies in the fact that the roots of crime are frequently embedded in early childhood experience. It is in childhood that personality develops and socialization patterns become established. Some experts are suggesting, therefore, that preventative measures to counter the growth of juvenile delinquency be expanded to include a greater focus on very young children and their families.

Although there has been an increase in juvenile delinquency in suburban areas in recent years, the greatest incidence is still considered to be centered in inner-city neighborhoods. There are several reasons for this. First of all, urban life is more conducive to crime because of greater social disorganization. Second, inner-city parents, struggling with poverty, are less able to spend time with their children and give them adequate supervision and emotional support. And lastly, the parents of a lower-class child who misbehaves do not have the same resources as do the parents of the middle-class child to cover up the offense so that it does not go on the public record.

The disparity between the number and the seriousness of crimes committed by adolescent boys and those committed by adolescent girls is narrowing, reflecting the increase in independent and aggressive behavior on the part of girls in our society. Drug use, too, is a factor; girls on hard drugs are likely to engage in thefts and prostitution to support their habit. Adolescent boys, too, are committing more drug-related crimes.

GROWING INTO MATURITY

The time at which the adolescent moves into adult mature status in modern society is different from place to place and from person to person.

Cultural Norms for Adult Status. Although the physical body furnishes many readily observed signals that the individual has stepped over the biological line between childhood and adulthood, our culture does not generally provide any clear-cut indication of the transition. Some societies still follow puberty customs which determine readiness and acceptance into the adult community. These "rites of passage" include endurance tests, physical feats of valor, and ritual dances. Although certain segments of modern society continue to observe such traditional reminders of their rites of passage as the Bar Mitzvah and Confirmation ceremonies, these are more symbolic than actual in the conferring of adulthood. Western society is more inclined to use chronological age, school placement, marriage, and degree of independence determined by work status as measures of maturity. Thus our initiation ceremonies might be said to be high school or college graduation and the test for a driver's license.

Legal Definition of Adulthood. Legal adulthood is conferred at different ages depending upon political jurisdiction. In the United States legal adulthood varies from state to state and can be as low as fourteen years of age and as high as twenty-one, although the national voting age is now eighteen. The distinction may also be defined in terms of the age at which an individual may join the army, vote, be served alcoholic beverages at a bar, and marry without parental consent.

Assumed Adult Status. Society tends to confer adult status upon an individual who has *assumed* adult status, regardless of his age or other legal definition of adulthood. Therefore, a person who lives in his or her own apartment, is fully employed, and is self-supporting is assumed to be an adult, particularly if he or she is married and has children. As a consequence young people from the lower socioeconomic brackets tend to move into adulthood earlier than their more affluent age-mates. This latter group remains financially dependent upon their parents well into their twenties as they pursue careers in colleges and universities.

Maturity. Chronological maturity is reached when a legal or cultural age level criterion is met. Physiological and mental maturity is reached when the physical and intellectual equipment of the person has developed fully. In this sense everyone who lives to reach these milestones achieves maturity. Adulthood and maturity, however, are not interchangeable terms. It is possible in our society to be physically mature yet emotionally and socially immature. Complete maturity is achieved when the individual (1) has reached the chronological age set by the society for adult status, (2) has reached physiological and mental maturity, and (3) has satisfactorily worked out the developmental tasks of adolescence.

References

1: The Study of Child Psychology

1. American Psychological Association: Committee on Ethical Standards in Psychological Research. "Ethical Standards for Research with Human Subjects," *APA Monitor,* May 1972, pp. I–XIX.
2. Aries, P. *Centuries of Childhood.* New York: Knopf, 1962.
3. Darwin, C. A. "A Biographical Sketch of an Infant," *Mind,* 1877, 2: 285–294.
4. Gesell, A., Halverson, H. M., Thompson, H., Ilg, F. L., Costner, B. M., Ames, L. B., and Amatruda, C. S. *The First Five Years of Life: A Guide to the Study of the Preschool Child.* New York: Harper & Row, 1940.
5. Greenleaf, B. K. *Children Through the Ages.* New York: McGraw Hill, 1978. Paper ed.: New York: Barnes & Noble, 1979.
6. Hall, G. S., "The Contents of Children's Minds on Entering School," *Pedagogical Seminary,* 1891, 1: 139–173.
7. Harlow, H. F. "Effects of Various Mother-Infant Relationships on Rhesus Monkey Behaviors," in B. M. Foss (ed.), *Determinants of Infant Behavior,* Vol. 4. New York: Barnes & Noble, 1969.
8. Locke, J. *Some Thoughts Concerning Education: 1690.* London: Cambridge University Press, 1913. Sections 38 and 40.
9. Mussen, P. H., Conger, J. J., and Kagen, J. *Child Development and Personality.* New York: Harper & Row, 1979. p. 13.
10. Rousseau, J. J. *Emile, or Concerning Education.* 1762. Book 2. New York: Dutton, 1938.
11. Society for Research in Child Development. Directory, 1977. 815 15th Street N.W., Washington, D.C., 20005.
12. Stone, L. *The Family, Sex, and Marriage in England, 1500–1800.* New York: Harper & Row, 1977.
13. Terman, L. M., and Merrill, M. A. *Measuring Intelligence: A Guide to the Administration of the New Revised Stanford-Binet Tests of Intelligence.* Boston: Houghton Mifflin, 1960.
14. Watson, J. B. *Psychology from the Standpoint of a Behaviorist.* Philadelphia: J. B. Lippincott, 1919.

15. Whitehurst, G. J., and Vasta, R. *Child Behavior.* Boston: Houghton Mifflin, 1977, pp. 39–40.

2: Principles and Theories of Development

1. Baldwin, A., *Theories of Development.* New York: John Wiley, 1967.
2. Bandura, A., and Walters, R. H. *Social Learning and Personality Development.* New York: Holt, Rinehart and Winston, 1963.
3. Bandura, A., Ross, D., and Ross, S. A. "Transmission of Aggression Through Imitation of Aggressive Models," *Journal of Abnormal and Social Psychology,* 1961, 63: 575–582.
4. Erikson, E., *Childhood and Society.* New York: W. W. Norton, 1963.
5. Freud, S., *Outline of Psychoanalysis.* New York: W. W. Norton, 1949.
6. Gesell, A., and Ames, L. B. *Youth: The Years from Ten to Sixteen.* New York: Harper & Brothers, 1956.
7. Gesell, A., Ilg, F. L., et al. *The Infant and the Child in the Culture of Today.* New York: Harper & Brothers, 1943.
8. Havighurst, R. J. *Human Development and Education.* New York: David McKay Co., 1953.
9. Harlow, H. F., and Suomi, S. J. "Nature of Love—Simplified," in Henry C. Lindgren (ed.), *Children's Behavior.* Palo Alto, Cal.: Mayfield Publishing Co., 1975, pp. 166–181.
10. Mead, M. *Growing up in New Guinea.* New York: Mentor Books, New American Library, 1953.
11. Pavlov, I. P. *Conditioned Reflexes.* London: Oxford University Press, 1928.
12. Piaget, J. "Piaget's Theory," in P. H. Mussen (ed.), *Manual of Psychology.* New York: John Wiley and Sons, 1970. Vol. 1, p. 703.
13. Pulaski, M. A. *Understanding Piaget.* New York: Harper & Row, 1971.
14. Sears, R. R. "A Theoretical Framework for Personality and Social Behavior," *American Psychologist,* 1951, 6: 476–483.
15. Sears, R. R., Rau, L., and Alpert, R. *Identification and Child Rearing.* Stanford, Cal.: Stanford University Press, 1965.
16. Skinner, B. F. *Science and Human Behavior.* New York: Macmillan, 1953.
17. Taussig, H. B. "The Thalidomide Syndrome," *Scientific American,* Aug. 1962, pp. 29–35.
18. Yarrow, L. J. "Separation from Parents During Early Childhood," in M. L. Hoffman and L. W. Hoffman (eds.), *Review of Child Development Research.* New York: Russell Sage Foundation, 1964, 1: 89–136.

3: Life Begins: Prenatal and Neonatal Development

1. Chess, S. "Temperament in the Normal Infant," in J. Hellmuth (ed.), *The Exceptional Infant,* Vol. 1. Seattle: Special Child Publications, 1967.
2. Colligan, D. "Tipping the Balance of the Sexes," *New York Magazine,* 1977, 10 (45): 65–73.

3. Conway, E., and Brackbill, Y. *Delivery Medication and Infant Outcome: An Empirical Study in the Effects of Obstetrical Medication on Fetus and Infant.* Monographs of the Society for Research in Child Development, 1970, 35: 24–34.
4. Dick-Read, G. *Childbirth Without Fear.* New York: Harper & Brothers, 1953.
5. *Environment, Heredity, and Intelligence* (1970), Reprint Series No. 2 of the *Harvard Educational Review.*
6. Fantz, R. L. "Pattern Vision in Newborn Infants," *Science,* 1963, 140: 296–297.
7. Jensen, A. R. "How Much Can We Boost IQ and Scholastic Achievement?" *Harvard Education Review,* 1969, 39: 1–123.
8. Lamaze, F. *Painless Childbirth.* London: Burke, 1958.
9. Leboyer, F. *Birth Without Violence.* New York: Random House, 1975.
10. Melnyk, J. M., and Koch, R. "Genetic Factors in Causation," in R. Koch and J. C. Dobson (eds.), *The Mentally Retarded Child and His Family.* New York: Brunner, Mazel, Butterworth, 1971, pp. 49–60.
11. Shank, R. E. "A Chink in Our Armor," *Nutrition Today,* 1970, 5(2): 2–11.
12. Sontag, L. W. "The Significance of Fetal Environmental Differences," *American Journal of Obstetrics and Gynecology,* 1941, 42: 996–1003.
13. Spitz, R., and Wolf, K. M. "Anaclitic Depression: An Inquiry into the Genesis of Psychiatric Conditions in Early Childhood," in A. Freud et al. (eds.), *The Psychoanalytic Study of the Child,* Vol. 2. New York: International Universities Press, 1946.
14. Thomas, A., Chess, S., Birch, M. G., Herzig, M. E., and Korn, S. *Behavioral Individuality in Early Childhood.* New York: New York University Press, 1963.
15. Vandenburg, S. G. "Hereditary Factors in Normal Personality Traits," in J. Wortis (ed.), *Recent Advances in Biological Psychiatry.* New York: Plenum Press, 1967, pp. 65–104.
16. Wolff, P. H. "Observations on the Early Development of Smiling," in B. M. Foss (ed.), *Determinants of Infant Behavior,* II. New York: John Wiley and Sons, 1963, pp. 113–138.
17. Ziegel, E., and Van Barcom, C. C. *Obstetric Nursing.* 6th ed. New York: Macmillan, 1972.

4: Infancy: The First Eighteen Months

1. Berry, J. W. "Temne and Eskimo Perceptual Skills," *International Journal of Psychology,* 1966, 1: 207–229.
2. Bloom, B. S. *Stability and Change in Human Characteristics.* New York: John Wiley and Sons, 1964.
3. Bowlby, J. *Attachment and Loss.* New York: Basic Books, Vol. 1, 1969; Vol. 2, 1973.
4. Bridges, K. M. "Emotional Development in Early Infancy," *Child Development,* 1932, 3: 340.

5. Brody, J. "New Studies Explain Protection Benefits of Mother's Milk," *New York Times,* Dec. 4, 1979, p. C1.
6. Caudill, W., and Plath, D. W. "Who Sleeps by Whom? Parent-Child Involvement in Urban Japanese Families," *Psychiatry,* 1966, 29: 344–366.
7. Erikson, E. H. *Childhood and Society.* New York: Norton, 1950.
8. Harlow, H. F. "Love in Infant Monkeys," *Scientific American,* 1959, 200: 68–74.
9. Hebb, D. O. *The Organization of Behavior.* New York: John Wiley and Sons, 1949.
10. Hunt, J. McV. *Intelligence and Experience.* New York: Ronald Press Book Co., 1961.
11. Kessen, W., Haith, M. W., and Salapatek, E. H. "Infancy," in P. H. Mussen (ed.), *Carmichael's Manual of Child Psychology.* New York: John Wiley and Sons, Inc., 1970, Vol. 1, pp. 304–306.
12. Lorenz, K. Z. *King Solomon's Ring.* New York: Thomas Crowell, 1952.
13. Piaget, J. *The Construction of Reality in the Child.* New York: Basic Books, 1954.
14. Spitz, R. A. "Hospitalism: An Inquiry into the Genesis of Psychiatric Conditions in Early Childhood," in A. Freud et al. (eds.), *The Psychoanalytic Study of the Child,* Vol. 1. New York: International Universities Press, 1945, pp. 53–74.
15. Thompson, W. R., and Grusec, J. E. "Studies of Early Experience," in P. H. Mussen (ed.), *Carmichael's Manual of Child Psychology.* New York: John Wiley and Sons, 1970, Vol. 1, pp. 565–654.
16. Walk, R. D. *The Development of Depth Perception in Animal and Human Infants.* Monographs of the Society for Research in Child Development, 1966, 31(5): 82–108.
17. White, B. L., and Watts, J. *Experience and Environment.* Englewood Cliffs, N.J.: Prentice Hall, 1973.

5: Toddlerhood Through the Preschool Years

1. Angrilli, A. "Psychosexual Identification of Preschool Boys," *Journal of Genetic Psychology,* 1960, 97: 329–340.
2. Bernstein, B. "Elaborated and Restricted Codes: Social Origins and Some Consequences," *American Anthropologist,* 1964, 64: 55–69.
3. Brown, R. *A First Language: The Early Stages.* Cambridge, Mass.: Harvard University Press, 1973.
4. Brown, R., Cazden, C., and Bellugi-Klima, U. "The Child's Grammar from I to III, in J. P. Hill (ed.), *Minnesota Symposia on Child Psychology,* Vol. 2. Minneapolis: University of Minnesota Press, 1969, p. 28.
5. Bruner, J. *Studies of Cognitive Growth.* New York: John Wiley and Sons, 1966.
6. Carroll, J. B. (ed.), *Language, Thought, and Reality: Selected Writings of Benjamin Whorf.* New York and Cambridge: Wiley and MIT Press, 1956.

7. Chomsky, N. *Language and Mind.* New York: Harcourt, Brace, Jovanovich, 1960.
8. Cicirelli, V. G., et al. *The Impact of Head Start: An Evaluation of the Effects of Head Start on Children's Cognitive and Affective Development,* Vols. 1 and 2. (Report to the Office of Economic Opportunity.) Athens, Ohio: Ohio University Press, 1969.
9. Eron, L. D. "Prescription for Reduction of Aggression," *American Psychologist,* March 1980, 35: 244–252.
10. Gaylin, W. *Feelings: Our Vital Signs.* New York: Harper & Row, 1979, p. 22.
11. Gesell, A., and Ilg, F. L. *Infant and Child in the Culture of Today.* New York: Harper & Row, 1943.
12. Hartup, W. W. "Peer Interaction and Social Organization," in Paul H. Mussen (ed.), *Carmichael's Manual of Child Psychology,* 3rd ed. Vol. II. New York: John Wiley and Sons, 1970, pp. 341–456.
13. Hetherington, E. M. "Sex Typing, Dependency, and Aggression," in T. D. Spencer and N. Kass (eds.), *Perspectives in Child Psychology.* New York: McGraw Hill, 1970.
14. Horowitz, R. E. "Spatial Localization of the Self," *Journal of Social Psychology,* 1935, 6: 379–387.
15. Jersild, A., and Holmes, F. B. *Children's Fears.* Child Development Monograph No. 20. New York: Columbia University Press, Teachers College, 1935.
16. Kagan, J., Kearsley, R. B., and Zelazo, P. R. "The Effects of Infant Day Care on Psychological Development," *Evaluation Quarterly.* Beverly Hills, Cal.: Sage Publications, Feb. 1977, pp. 109–142.
17. McGuinness, D., and Pribram, K. "The Origins of Sensory Bias in the Development of Gender Differences in Perception and Cognition," in Morton Bortner (ed.), *Cognitive Growth and Development.* New York: Brunner/Mazel, 1979.
18. McNeill, D. *The Acquisition of Language.* New York: Harper & Row, 1970.
19. McNeill, D. "The Development of Language," in P. Mussen (ed.), *Carmichael's Manual of Child Psychology,* Vol. I. New York: John Wiley, 1970, pp. 1061–1161.
20. Palmer, F. H. *The Effects of Early Childhood Educational Intervention.* Paper Prepared for the President's Commission on Mental Health, July 1977.
21. Skinner, B. F. *Verbal Behavior.* New York: Appleton-Century-Crofts, 1957.
22. Smart, M. S., and Smart, R. C. *Children.* New York: Macmillan Co., 1970.
23. Swift, J. "Effects of Early Group Experience: The Nursery School and Day Nursery," in M. L. Hoffman and L. Wladis (eds.), *Review of Child Development Research,* Vol. I. New York: Russell Sage Foundation, 1964, pp. 249–288.

24. Thompson, W. R., and Grusec, J. E. "Studies of Early Experience," in P. H. Mussen (ed.), *Carmichael's Manual of Child Psychology*, Vol. I. New York: John Wiley, 1976, pp. 565–654.
25. Trotter, R. J. "Environment and Behavior: Intensive Intervention Program Prevents Retardation." (The Milwaukee Project.) *APA Monitor*, American Psychological Association, Sept.–Oct., 1976, p. 4.
26. Vaughan, V. "Developmental Pediatrics," in W. E. Nelson (ed.), *Textbook of Pediatrics*. Philadelphia: W. B. Saunders, 1979, chap. 2.

6: The Middle Years

1. Altus, W. D. "Birth Order and Its Sequelae," *Science*, 1966, 151: 44–49.
2. Baumrind, D. "Child Care Practices Anteceding Three Patterns of Preschool Behavior," *Genetic Psychology*, 1967, 75: 43–88.
3. Bronfenbrenner, U. *Two Worlds of Childhood: U.S. and U.S.S.R.* New York: Simon and Schuster, 1972.
4. Bruner, J. *Toward a Theory of Instruction*. Cambridge, Mass.: Harvard University Press, 1968.
5. Bruner, J., Oliver, R. R., and Greenfield, P. M. *Studies in Cognitive Growth*. New York: John Wiley, 1966.
6. Coleman, J. S., et al. *Equality of Educational Opportunity*. Washington, D.C.: U.S. Government Printing Office, 1966.
7. Gesell, A., and Armatruda, C. S. *Developmental Diagnosis*. New York: Paul Hober, 1947.
8. Goodman, P. *Compulsory Mis-Education*. New York: Horizon Press, 1964.
9. Guilford, J. P. "The Structure of Intellect," *Psychological Bulletin*, 1956, 53: 267–293.
10. Havighurst, R. G. *Human Development and Education*. New York: David McKay Co., 1953.
11. Heilbrun, A. B., Jr. "Parental Model Attributes, Nurturant Reinforcement, and Consistency of Behavior in Adolescence," *Child Development*, 1964, 35: 151–167.
12. Helfat, L. "The Gut Level Needs of Kids," *Learning*, 1973, 2: 30–34.
13. Hilgard, E. R., and Bower, G. H. *Theories of Learning*. New York: Appleton-Century-Crofts, 1966.
14. Horowitz, F. D. "The Relationship of Anxiety, Self-Concept, and Sociometric Status Among Fourth, Fifth, and Sixth Grade Children," *Journal of Abnormal and Social Psychology*, 1962, 65: 212–214.
15. Illich, I. *Deschooling Society*. New York: Harper & Row, 1971.
16. Jencks, C. S. *Inequality: A Reassessment of the Effect of Family and Schooling in America*. New York: Basic Books, 1972.
17. Koch, H. L. "The Relation in Young Children Between Characteristics of Their Playmates and Certain Attributes of Their Siblings," *Child Development*, 1957, 28: 175–202.

18. Kohlberg, L. *Stages in the Development of Moral Thought.* New York: Holt, Rinehart and Winston, 1969.
19. Kubie, L. "The Child's Fifth Freedom," in Child Study Association of America (ed.), *Our Children Today.* New York: Viking Press, 1952, p. 146.
20. Lewin, K., Lippett, R., and White, R. K. "Patterns of Aggressive Behavior in Experimentally Created 'Social Climates,'" *Journal of Social Psychology,* 1939, 10: 271–290.
21. McCandless, B. R., and Trotter, R. J. *Children.* New York: Holt, Rinehart and Winston, 1977.
22. Mead, M. *Sex and Temperament in Three Primitive Societies.* New York: New American Library, 1935.
23. Neill, A. S. *Summerhill.* New York: Hart, 1960, p. 4.
24. Newsletter of the New York State Psychological Association, Division of School Psychology, 1970, 14 (2), 5.
25. Piaget, J. *The Moral Judgement of The Child.* New York: Harcourt Brace, 1932.
26. Samuda, R. J. *Psychological Testing of American Minorities.* New York: Dodd, Mead, and Co., 1975.
27. Terman, L., and Merrill, M. A. *Stanford-Binet Intelligence Scale.* Boston: Houghton Mifflin, 1960.
28. Thurstone, L. L. *Primary Mental Abilities.* Psychometric Monographs, 1938, No. 1.
29. Wechsler, D. *Measurement of Adult Intelligence.* Baltimore: Williams and Wilkins Co., 1947, p. 3.
30. Wechsler, D. *Manual for the Wechsler Intelligence Scale for Children—Revised.* New York: Psychological Corp., 1974.

7: Adolescence

1. Bachman, J., Green, S., and Wirtanen, I. *Youth in Transition,* Vol. III: *Dropping Out—Problem or Symptom?* Ann Arbor: Survey Research Center, Institute for Social Research, 1971.
2. Bakan, D. "Adolescence in America," *Daedalus,* 1971, 100: 975–995.
3. Blount, J. H., Darrow, W. W., and Johnson, R. E. "Venereal Disease in Adolescents," *Pediatric Clinics of North America,* Nov. 1973, 20: 1021–1033.
4. Dixon, M. C., and Wright, W. E. *Juvenile Delinquency Prevention Program.* Nashville, Tenn.: Office of Educational Services, Peabody College for Teachers, 1975.
5. Faust, M. S. "Developmental Maturity as a Detriment in Prestige of Adolescent Girls," *Child Development,* 1960, 31: 173–184.
6. Ginsburg, H., and Opper, S. *Piaget's Theory of Intellectual Development.* Englewood Cliffs, N.J.: Prentice Hall, 1969.
7. Hall, G. S. *Adolescence.* New York: Appleton, 1904.

8. Hamill, P. V. V., Dried, T. A., Johnson, C. L., Reed, R. B., and Roche, A. F. *Health Examination Survey Data.* From the National Center for Health Statistics, U.S. Department of Health, Education, and Welfare. Rockville, Md.: June 1976. (HRA) 76-1120, Vol. 25, No. 3.
9. Jacobs, J. *Adolescent Suicide.* New York: Wiley Interscience, 1971.
10. Jones, M. C. "A Study of Socialization Patterns at the High School Level," *Journal of Educational Psychology,* 1950, 41: 129–148.
11. Kantner, J. F., and Zelnik, M. "Sexual Experience of Young Married Women in the United States," *Family Planning Perspectives,* 1972, 4: 9–18.
12. Kett, J. F. *Rites of Passage: Adolescence in America, 1790 to the Present.* New York: Basic Books, 1977.
13. Mead, M. *Coming of Age in Samoa.* New York: Morrow, 1961.
14. Rosenberg, M. *Society and the Adolescent Self-Image.* Princeton, N.J.: Princeton University Press, 1965.
15. Schmeck, H. M., Jr. "Trend in Growth of Children Lags," *New York Times,* June 10, 1976, p. 13.
16. Shenker, I. R., and Schildkrout, M. *Physical and Emotional Health of Youth.* The Seventy-Fourth Yearbook of the National Society for the Study of Education. Youth Part 1. Chicago: University of Chicago Press, 1975.
17. Sorenson, R. C. *Adolescent Sexuality in Contemporary America.* New York: World Publishing Co., 1973.
18. Toffler, A. *Future Shock.* New York: Random House, 1970.
19. Weatherly, D. "Self-Perceived Rate of Physical Maturation and Personality in Late Adolescence," *Child Development,* 1964, 35: 1197–1210.

Index

accommodation, in Piagetian theory, 24, 58
activity levels, 34, 35, 61
　aggression and, 97
adjustment problems:
　in adolescence, 156–160
　in childhood, 138–142
Adler, Alfred, 6, 28
adolescence, 49, 129, 143–162
　adjustment problems in, 156–160
　clarification of goals in, 143, 150–151
　as "created" and "discovered," 152–153
　defined, 143
　generation gap and, 149, 153–154
　growing into maturity in, 146, 160–162
　growth spurt in, 144–145, 148–149
　mental development in, 110, 146–148
　personality development in, 144, 148–152
　physical development in, 14, 51, 52, 108, 144–146, 148–149, 156
　social development in, 144, 152–156
　tasks of, 143–144, 149–152
　values development in, 143, 151–152
adolescent medicine, 1–2
adulthood, 17, 160–162
　assumption of, 161
　cultural norms for, 160–161
　legal definition of, 161
　maturity vs., 161–162
aggression, 18, 25, 96–98
　expression of, 96–97, 102
　origins of, 97–98, 127
alcohol, 158–159
　prenatal development affected by, 39–40
Alpha Fetal Protein test (AFP), 37
American Academy of Pediatrics, 109
American Psychological Association, 11

Ames, Louise, 22
amniocentesis, 32, 37
amniotic sac, 37
anal stage, in Freudian theory, 27, 92
anemia, 33, 40
anesthesia, 41, 42
anorexia nervosa, 157
anoxia, 42–43
anxiety, 67, 96, 104, 128, 132, 133–134
　birth trauma and, 47–48
　castration, 27, 98
　defense mechanisms and, 26–27, 147–148
　stranger, 69
Apgar score, 41
aphasia, 138
Aristotle, 2
assimilation, in Piagetian theory, 24, 57–58
associative play, defined, 101–102
auditory perception, 55–56
autism, 100
autonomy stage, in personality development, 91–92

babbling, 60, 77, 81
Babinski reflex, 45, 56
Bandura, Albert, 21
bed-wetting, 105
behaviorism, 5, 20, 72, 104
Bender-Gestalt Visual Motor Test, 128
Benedict, Ruth, 129
Bernstein, Basil, 83
Besell and Palomares Human Development Program, 137
Binet, Alfred, 4
Binet-Simon tests, 4, 116
Biographical Sketch of an Infant (Darwin), 3

INDEX

birth, 30, 41–43, 138
   injuries at, 42–43
   process of, 41–42
birth control, 155, 156
birth trauma, 47–48
blastocyst, defined, 37
blindness, 33, 40, 42, 43
Bloom, Benjamin, 68
body proportions:
   in infancy, 51, 61
   in middle years, 108
   in toddlerhood through preschool years, 73, 74–75
Boston Kindergarten Studies (Hall), 4
bottle feeding, 71–72
Bowlby, John, 48, 64–65, 67
boys, *see* girls and boys, comparisons of
breast-feeding, 71–72
breech births, 41
Bridges, K. M., 67
Bronfenbrenner, Uri, 133
Brown, Roger, 81–82
Bruner, Jerome, 85, 111–112

Caudill, W., 71
castration anxiety, 27, 98
cathexis, 25
central nervous system, in infancy, 52–53
cephalo-caudal principle, 15, 51
cerebral palsy, 43
Chess, Stella, 35
child psychology:
   historical review of, 2–6
   importance of, 1–2
   improvements in status of children and, 5–6
   methods of study in, 6–12
   principles of development in, 13–18
   role of theory in, 18–19
   theories of development in, 19–29
Children's Manifest Anxiety Scale (CMAS), 128
child studies, 6–12
   approaches to, 9–11
   ethics of, 11–12
   settings for, 8–9
Chomsky, Noam, 79–80
chorion, defined, 37
chromosomes, 30–32, 37
   sex, 31–32, 35
circulation, neonate, 44, 46

class differences:
   adolescent adjustment problems and, 158, 159, 160
   age of adulthood and, 161
   infant social development and, 70–71
   intelligence tests and, 116, 119–121
   language acquisition and, 78, 83
   school performance and, 134
classical conditioning, 20–21
classification, in mental development, 23, 113
clinical methods, types of, 7
CMAS (Children's Manifest Anxiety Scale), 128
cognition:
   deprivation and enrichment as influences on, 88–90
   in infancy, 56–59
   intelligence and, *see* intelligence
   language acquisition and, 78–79
   in middle years, 110–113
   moral development related to, 121–124
   psychosexual identification and, 99–100
   in toddlerhood through preschool years, 73–74, 84–90
   units of, 56–57, 85–87
cognitive stage theory, *see* Piaget, Jean, and Piagetian theory
Coleman, James, 134
colic, maternal tension and, 39, 46
colostrum, 46
Comenius, John Amos, 3
competition, sex and, 108, 127
conception, 30, 31–32, 37, 138
concepts, as unit of cognition, 85–86, 87, 110
concrete operations stage, in cognitive development theory, 23, 88, 109, 112–113, 122, 147
conditioning:
   classical, 20–21
   operant, 5, 21, 79
   S-R and, 5, 20–22
conservation principle, concrete operations period and, 23, 113
cooperative play, 102
creeping, 50, 53
cross-sectional approach to child study, 10–11
cross-sectional/longitudinal approach to child study, 11

INDEX

crushes, adolescent, 154–155
culture, 17–18
  generation gap and, 153–154
  infant development influenced by, 33–34, 62–63, 70–71
  intelligence tests and, 119–121
  language acquisition influenced by, 77–78
  norms for adulthood and, 160–161
  social development influenced by, 129–130

Darwin, Charles, 3
deafness, 40, 43, 60, 77
deep structure, defined, 80
defense mechanisms, 26–27, 147–148
denial, 26
deoxyribonucleic acid (DNA), 31
dependent variables, 7–8
depression, 34, 68
  in adolescence, 156–157
deprivation, early, 68
depth perception, 55
developmental tasks, 16–17
development and growth, 13–29
  asynchronous, 15, 51, 145
  continuity and discontinuity in, 14–15
  critical periods of, 16, 17, 38, 39
  cultural determinants of, 17–18, 62–63, 70–71, 77–78, 119–121, 129–130, 160–161
  gradients, 15
  imprinting and, 17
  individual differences in, 15–16
  maturation as characteristic of, 13–14
  mental, *see* mental development
  of personality, *see* personality development
  physical, *see* physical development
  predictable patterns of, 15
  principles of, 13–18
  social, *see* social development
  theories of, 19–29
Dewey, John, 5
diabetes mellitus, 33, 40, 105
Dick-Read, Grantly, 41
differentiation, defined, 15
diphtheria, 109
discontinuity of growth rate, defined, 14–15, 51
displacement, 27
DNA (deoxyribonucleic acid), 31

Dollard, John, 21
Down's syndrome, 32, 33, 35
dreams, 45, 95
dropouts, 157–158
drugs, 6
  adolescents and, 153, 158–159
  prenatal development influenced by, 33, 38, 39
dyslexia, 121, 138

education, 5, 18, 34
  adolescent problems and, 157–159
  classroom climate in, 135
  desegregation of, 135
  learning disabilities and, 138–139
  mental retardation and, 140–141
  in middle years, 107, 109, 129, 133–139, 141–142
  parental encouragement and, 133–134
  in preschool period, 88–90, 103–104
  school phobia and, 141–142
  sex, 137–138, 155, 156
  teacher-pupil relations and, 135–137, 141
educational psychology, 4, 136–137
ego, 26–27
Electra complex, 28
embryonic stage of prenatal growth, 37–38
Emile (Rousseau), 3
emotional learning, 136–137
emotions:
  in infancy, 65–67
  neonatal development and, 47–48
  in personality development, 65–67, 95–98
  prenatal development influenced by, 39, 42
enactive representation, cognition and, 111–112
endocrine glands, in adolescence, 144
equilibration, in Piagetian theory, 24, 58
Erikson, Erik, 6, 28–29, 64, 67, 91–93
existential theories, 29
experimental groups, 8

fathers, as role models, 22, 27
fears, 95–96, 104
  of school, 141–142
  see also anxiety
feeding, *see* nutrition and feeding

feminist movement, sex roles affected by, 151
fetal stage of prenatal growth, 38
fetus, environmental influences on, 38–41
field theory, 29
Figure Drawing tests, 7, 128
fixation, 28
fontanels, 47, 52
fraternal twins, 33, 34
Freud, Sigmund, 6, 24–28, 67
  see also psychoanalytic theory
Fromm, Erich, 28
frustration-aggression hypothesis, 97

Galton, Francis, 4
gametes, 31–32
Gaylin, W., 96
generation gap, 149, 153–154
genes and genetics:
  aggression and, 98
  diseases and disorders of, 32, 33, 35–37, 141
  dominant, 32
  in language acquisition, 82–83
  laterality and, 76
  prenatal development influenced by, 30–37
  recessive, 32, 35
gene-splicing, 31
genital stage, in Freudian theory, 28
German measles, 40, 109
Gesell, Arnold, 4, 6, 22, 76
gestation period, 37–41
girls and boys, comparisons of
  aggression in, 97–98, 127
  body build in, 108
  crime patterns in, 160
  drug use in, 159
  height in, 51, 74, 107–108, 144–145
  motor coordination in, 108–109
  play in, 103
  sexual views of, 154, 155
  teeth development in, 52
  toilet training in, 105
  weight in, 144–145
gonorrhea, 40, 155–156
Goodman, Paul, 135
group pressure, 131–132
growth, *see* development and growth
Guilford, J. P., 115

habituation:
  in infancy, 57, 67
  in neonates, 47
Hall, G. Stanley, 4, 22, 153, 156
Harlow, Harry, 6, 12, 16, 65
Harvard University Center for Educational Policy Research, 135
Havighurst, Robert, 16–17, 107, 125
Hebb, D. O., 68
Heber, Rick, 89
height, 33, 34
  in adolescence, 144–145, 146
  in infancy, 50–51, 61
  in middle years, 106–107
  in toddlerhood through preschool years, 74
hemophilia, 33
hemophilus vaginalis, 156
heredity, *see* genes and genetics
heroin, prenatal development and, 39
herpes progenitalis, 156
Holmes, F. B., 95
holophrases, 81
homosexuality, 28, 98, 138, 151
hormones, 14, 98, 144, 145
Horney, Karen, 28
HTP test, 128
Hull, Clark L., 20–21
humanistic psychology, 29

id, defined, 26
identical twins, 33, 34
ikonic representation, cognition and, 85, 112
Ilg, Francis, 22
Illich, Ivan, 135
images, as units of cognition, 57, 85
imaginary playmates, 102–103
immunity:
  breast-feeding and, 71
  of neonates, 47
imprinting, defined, 17
independence:
  in adolescence, 143, 149–150
  peer influences on, 131, 149
independent variables, 7
infancy, 49–72
  attachment and dependence in, 64–65
  immunization in, 109
  mental development in, 33–34, 50, 53–61, 111–112
  perception in, 54–56

INDEX

infancy *(cont'd)*
  personality development in, 61–69
  physical development in, 49–53
  social development in, 69–72
infections, 33, 42, 47
influenza, 40
information-processing theory, 111–112
  initiative stage, in personality development, 92–93
instrumental learning, 21
intellectualization, as defense mechanism, 27, 147–148
intelligence, 113–121
  defined, 113, 114–115
  as general or "g" factor, 115
  heredity vs. environment in determination of, 33–34, 121
  nature of, 114, 115
  popularity and, 104
  specific or "s" factors in, 115
intelligence quotient (IQ):
  computation of, 117, 118, 121
  mental retardation and, 140
intelligence tests, 4, 83, 115–121
  Binet-Simon, 4, 116
  critique of, 119–121
  group, 119
  Standard English and, 120
  standardization of, 116
  Stanford-Binet, 4, 114–115, 116–117, 118
  Wechsler, 117–119
introspective reportage, 6
introspective thinking, 148

jaundice, neonate, 44, 46
Jencks, Christopher, 134, 135
Jensen, Arthur, 34
Jersild, A., 95
Johnson, Lyndon, 88
Jung, Carl, 6, 28
juvenile delinquency, 142, 158, 159–160

Kagan, J., 90
Kearsley, R. B., 90
Klinefelter's syndrome, 35
Kohlberg, Lawrence, 6, 99–100
  on moral development stages, 122–123
Kubie, Lawrence, 137

laboratory setting, 9
labor pains, 41

Lamaze, Fernand, 41
language, 126
  intelligence tests and, 117, 118, 119, 120
  uses of, 83–84
language acquisition:
  factors in, 77–79, 82–84
  gradual increase of skills and, 80–82
  in infancy, 50, 60–61, 70, 73
  theories of, 79–80
  timing of, 60, 77, 81–82
  transformational rules and, 80
  in toddlerhood through preschool years, 73, 74, 77–84
Language Acquisition Device (LAD), 80
language codes, restricted vs. elaborated, 83
latency stage, in Freudian theory, 28, 106, 124, 137
latency years, *see* middle years
laterality, in physical development, 76
learning:
  emotional, 136–137
  in infancy, 59–60
  of languages, *see* language acquisition
  in psychosexual identification, 99
  theories of, 19–22, 111
  see also education; mental development
learning disabilities, 138–139, 157
Leboyer, Frederick, 42
left-handedness, 76
Lewin, Kurt, 29, 136
libido, in Freudian theory, 25
Lippett, R., 136
Locke, John, 3
locomotion, in physical development, 76
longitudinal approach to child study, 7, 9–10
Lorenz, Konrad, 64
LSD, prenatal development and, 39

McCandless, B. R., 111
McNeill, David, 77, 78, 80
mainstreaming, 139
marasmus, 48
marijuana, 159
Maslow, Abraham, 29
maturation, 13–14, 107, 160–162
  language acquisition and, 78
  sexual, 144, 145–146, 152–153
  social trends and, 146
maturation theory, 22

MBD (minimal brain dysfunction), 43, 138
Mead, Margaret, 17, 129
mean length of utterance (MLU), 81–82
measles, 109
meconium, in neonates, 46
meiosis, 31
Mendel, Gregor, 32
menstruation, 14, 144, 145–146
mental development:
  in adolescence, 110, 146–148
  in infancy, 33–34, 50, 53–61, 111–112
  in middle years, 109–124
  schemata in, 24, 56–57, 58, 85
  in toddlerhood through preschool years, 73–74, 77–90, 112
  use of concepts in, 85–86, 87, 110
  use of symbols in, 85, 110, 112–113
  see also cognition; intelligence
mental retardation, 38, 40, 116, 139–141
  causes of, 141
  degrees of, 140
  Down's syndrome and, 32, 33, 35
middle years, 49, 106–142
  adjustment problems of, 138–142
  childhood diseases in, 109
  growth rate in, 107–108
  mental development in, 109–124
  moral development in, 23–24, 121–124, 133
  moral relativism in, 24, 122
  personality development in, 124–128
  physical development in, 106–109
  social development in, 128–138, 153
milk teeth, 52
Miller, Neal, 21
Milwaukee Project, 89, 90
minimal brain dysfunction (MBD), 43, 138
Minnesota Multiphasic Personality Inventory (MMPI), 128
miscarriages, 38
mitosis, 30–31
MLU (mean length of utterance), 81–82
MMPI (Minnesota Multiphasic Personality Inventory), 128
modeling, 18
  in psychosexual identification, 22, 27–28, 99
monkeys, studies of, 12, 16, 65
Montessori, Maria, 5
moral development, 121–124, 133, 138

Moro reflex, 44, 45
morphemes, 80
mothers, 12
  in childbirth process, 41–42
  infant development and, 62–63
  neonatal stage and, 17, 19, 45, 48
  prenatal development and, 33, 38–41
motor development:
  in infancy, 53, 62
  in middle years, 106, 107, 108–109
  in neonates, 45–46
  in toddlerhood through preschool years, 73, 75–76
mumps, 40, 109

National Center for Health Statistics, U.S., 146
National Institute of Alcohol Abuse and Alcoholism, 40
natural childbirth, 41–42
natural setting and experiment for child studies, 8
nature-nurture controversy, 32–35
  intelligence and, 33–34, 121
  personality and, 34–35
  see also class differences; culture; genes and genetics
Neill, A. S., 135
neonatal period, 17, 43–48, 49
  emotional response in, 47–48
  physical development in, 44–47
New Guinea, child development in, 17, 129
nondirective approach to development, 29
nutrition and feeding, 14, 33, 146, 157
  in infancy, 51–52, 71–72
  for neonates, 44, 45, 46
  PKU and, 35–37
  prenatal development influenced by, 33, 38–39, 42
  in toddlerhood and preschool years, 75

object permanence, 55
observation tests, 127, 128
Oedipus complex, 27, 93, 98–99, 123
On the Origin of Species (Darwin), 3
open classrooms, 135
operant conditioning, 5, 21, 79
oral stage, in Freudian theory, 27, 28, 64
ovum, 31–32, 37, 146

INDEX

Palmer, Francis, 89–90
paper-and-pencil tests, 127, 128
parallel play, 101
parents, 18, 133
   adolescent adjustment problems and, 157, 158–159, 160
   child psychology as aid to, 1, 5–6
   genetics and, 30, 32
   personality development influenced by, 61, 62–65, 94, 99, 125–127, 150
   sex education as viewed by, 137–138
   see also fathers; mothers
pattern perception, 55
Pavlov, Ivan, 5, 20
peer relationships, 17, 18
   in adolescence, 129, 143, 149, 154–156, 157
   of infants, 70, 73
   in middle years, 107, 129, 130–132
   selectivity and, 131–132
   in toddlerhood through preschool years, 73, 103, 104
penis envy, 28, 98–99
perception, 138
   in infancy, 54–56
personality development:
   in adolescence, 144, 148–152
   constitutional determinants of, 61–62, 148–149
   cultural determinants of, 62–63, 95
   disorders in, 100
   effects of early life experiences on, 67–69
   Erikson on stages of, 91–93
   family influences on, 61, 62–65, 94, 99, 125–127, 150
   Freudian theory of, *see* psychoanalytic theory
   heredity vs. environment in determination of, 34–35
   in infancy, 61–69
   interpersonal determinants of, 61, 62–65, 68–69, 94, 125–127, 149–150
   in middle years, 124–128
   situational or accidental determinants of, 63
   in toddlerhood through preschool years, 90–100
personality testing, 127–128
Pestalozzi, Heinrich, 3

phallic stage, in Freudian theory, 27–28, 93
phenylketonuria (PKU), 33, 35–57
phonemes, 80
physical development:
   in adolescence, 14, 51, 52, 108, 144–146, 148–149, 156
   in infancy, 49–53
   in middle years, 106–109
   in neonatal period, 44–47
   in toddlerhood through preschool years, 73, 74–77
Piaget, Jean, and Piagetian theory, 6, 22–24, 55
   concrete operations stage in, 23, 88, 109–110, 112–113, 122, 147
   formal operations stage in, 23–24, 110, 147
   language as viewed by, 82, 84
   moral development in, 23–24, 121–122, 123
   preoperational stage in, 23, 87–88, 122
   sensorimotor stage in, 23, 57–59
PKU (phenylketonuria), 33, 35–37
placenta, 37, 39, 41, 46
Plath, D. W., 71
Plato, 2
play, 24, 101–103, 107, 130
   functions of, 102–103
pleasure principle, 26
polio, 40, 109
popularity, 104, 131
PPM (psychoprophylactic method), 41
pregnancy, adolescent, 146, 155
prematurity, 38, 42
prenatal development, 30–41, 49
   environmental influences on, 38–41
   genetic influences on, 30–37
   mother's age and, 38
   stages of, 37–38
preoperational stage, in cognitive development theory, 23, 87–88, 122
preschool years, *see* toddlerhood through preschool years
Preyer, Wilhelm, 3
Project Head Start, 88
projection, 26–27
projective techniques, 127, 128
proximo-distal principle, 15
psychoanalytic (Freudian) theory:
   anal stage in, 27, 92
   genital stage in, 28

psychoanalytic (Freudian) theory: (cont'd)
 latency stage in, 28, 106, 124, 137
 oral stage in, 27, 28, 64
 phallic stage in, 27–28, 93
 toilet training as viewed in, 27, 75, 91, 92
psychophophylactic method (PPM), 41
psychoses, 100
psychosexual stages of development, see psychoanalytic theory
psychosocial stages of development (Erickson), 28–29, 64, 67, 91–93
puberty, 144, 145–146, 152–153, 161
punishment, 122, 126, 150, 157

radiation, prenatal abnormality and, 38, 40
Rank, Otto, 47–48
rapid eye movements (REM), 45
rationalization, 26
reality principle, 26
recombinant DNA technology, 31
reflexes:
 of infants, 56, 69
 of neonates, 44–45, 48
reinforcement theory of language acquisition, 79
repression, 26
Republic, The (Plato), 2
respiration, neonate, 46, 47
retrolental fibroplasia, 42
reversibility, cognitive development and, 23, 113
Rh factor, prenatal development and, 40–41
Ribble, Margaret, 48
right-handedness, 76
Rogers, Carl, 29
rooting reflex, 44, 45
Rorschach inkblots, 7, 128
Rousseau, Jean Jacques, 3
rubella, 40, 109

schemata, in infancy, 56–57, 58, 85
schizophrenia, 100
School of Infancy (Comenius), 3
school phobia, 141–142
Sears, Robert, 21
self-awareness, development of, 93
self-concept, 93–95
 in adolescence, 143, 148, 150–151

self-concept (cont'd)
 determinants of, 94–95, 131–132
 importance of, 93–94
senses:
 of infants, 54–56
 of neonates, 47
sensorimotor stage, in cognitive development theory, 23, 57–59
seriation, cognitive development and, 113
sex chromosomes, 31–32, 35
sex discrimination, 108
sex education, 137–138, 155, 156
sexual development:
 in adolescence, 143, 144, 145–146, 149, 153, 154–156, 157
 latency period and, 28, 106, 124, 137
 in middle years, 124–125, 130
 role formation in, 6, 17, 27–28, 98–100, 125, 143, 151–152
 secondary sex characteristics and, 145, 149
sibling influences, 63, 64, 127, 133
sickle-cell anemia, 33
Simon, Theophile, 4
skeletal structure:
 in infancy, 52, 62
 in neonates, 47
 in toddlerhood through preschool years, 75
Skinner, B. F., 5, 21, 79
sleep habits, neonate, 45
smile reflex, 48, 69
smoking:
 in adolescence, 158–159
 prenatal development and, 40, 42
Snellen scale, 54
social development:
 in adolescence, 144, 152–156
 family influences on, 70–71, 104–105, 132–134, 153, 154
 in infancy, 69–72
 language as vehicle of, 84
 in middle years, 128–138, 153
 play in, 101–103, 107, 130
 in toddlerhood through preschool years, 101–105, 128–129
social learning theory, 21–22
Society of Research in Child Development, 11
Spence, Kenneth, 20–21
sperm, 31–32, 37
 at puberty, 144, 145–146

INDEX

sphincter muscles, 14, 75
Spitz, René, 48
S-R (stimulus and response), 5, 20–22
stage theories, 19, 22–29
  cognitive, *see* Piaget, Jean, and Piagetian theory
  psychosexual, *see* psychoanalytic theory
  psychosocial (Erikson), 28–29, 64, 67, 91–93
Stanford-Binet Intelligence Test, 4, 114–115, 116–117, 118
Stephens, J. M., 134
Stern, William, 116
stillbirths, 38
stimulation, early, 68–69
stimulus and response (S-R), 5, 20–22
structural theory, 111, 112–113
sucking reflex, 44, 45
suicide, in adolescence, 156–157
Sullivan, Harry Stack, 28
Summerhill (Neill), 135
superego, 26, 92–93, 133
surface structure, 80
swallowing reflex, 44, 45
symbols, as unit of cognition, 85, 110, 112–113
syntax, 77, 79, 80, 81, 82
syphilis, 40

TAT (Thematic Apperception Test), 7, 128
Tay-Sachs disease, 32
teeth, in infancy, 52
telegraphic speech, 81
temperature regulation, neonate, 44, 46–47
Terman, Lewis, 4, 116
tetanus, 109
thalidomide, 39
Thematic Apperception Test (TAT), 7, 128
therapy, 19, 100, 142
third-force psychology, 29
Thomas, Alexander, 48
Thorndike, Edward, 20–21
Thurstone, L. L., 115
Tiedemann, Dieterich, 3
toddlerhood through preschool years, 49, 73–105
  biological changes in, 74–75

toddlerhood through preschool years *(cont'd)*
  biological changes in, 74–75
  cognition in, 84–90
  environmental influences on growth in, 75
  expansion of motor skills in, 75–76
  language development in, 77–84
  mental development in, 73–74, 77–90, 112
  moral realism in, 24, 122
  personality development in, 90–100
  physical development in, 73, 74–76
  social development in, 101–105, 128–129
toilet training, 27, 75, 91–92, 126
  socialization and, 104–105
toxemia, 40
transformational rules, 80
transsexuals, 98
trichomiasis, 156
trophoblast, 37
Trotter, R. J., 111
trust, development of, 64, 67
Turner's syndrome, 35
twins, 33, 34

umbilical cords, 37, 41, 42, 44
unconscious, Freudian view of, 25–26
underachievement, in adolescence, 157
United States Commission on Civil Rights, 88–89
uterus, 37, 41, 46

vaccination, 109
values, crystallization of, in adolescence, 143, 151–152
Vasta, R., 11
venereal disease, 40, 138, 155–156
visual perception, 54–55
vocalization, 70, 81

Walk-Gibson visual cliff experiments, 55
walking, 50, 53, 73
Watson, John B., 5, 6, 20, 104
Wechsler, David, 114, 117
Wechsler intelligence scales, 117–119
weight:
  in adolescence, 144–145, 151
  in infancy, 51–52, 61
  of neonates, 42, 44, 46
  in toddlerhood through preschool years, 74–75

White, Burton, 68
White, R. K., 136
Whitehurst, G. J., 11
whooping cough, 109
Whorf, Benjamin Lee, 78–79, 84

Wolff, Peter, 48
World in Pictures, The (Comenius), 3

Zelazo, P. R., 90
zygotes, 31, 37